ADVANCED PRAISE FOR *THIS IS YOUR CAPTAIN SPEAKING*

"Captain O'Shaughnessy gives us a rare, up-close, and honest look at the challenges that airline pilots face by bravely and boldly sharing her journey. The powerful insights and solutions she offers will serve as a lifeline for many. Whether you are a pilot or passenger, you will benefit from this book!"

— Dr. Amishi Jha,
professor and director of Contemplative Neuroscience,
University of Miami

"An important work on a long-overdue subject. Capt. O' pulls back the curtain on the subject of mental health and well-being in the aviation profession. Pilots, ATC professionals, and cabin crew are in the midst of a mental health crises in an industry that largely refuses to acknowledge, or have meaningful dialog about it. Tragically, most who suffer will never seek help or even bring up the subject for fear of losing their job. Punishing those who self-disclose simply drives the problem underground while creating more, not less, depression and anxiety. This book is for anyone concerned about the 'human factors' that keep airliners operating safely."

— Carl Eisen,
A300 captain (retired), UCLA-trained Mindfulness Facilitator,
IMTA-P, and founder of Mindful Aviator

"*This Is Your Captain Speaking* offers an eloquently constructed inquiry into the role of outdated views and ineffective approaches to pilot wellness and how it negatively impacts human suffering and aviation safety."

— Captain Matthew C. McNeil, MS, LPC, ATP,
founder and clinical director of LiftAffect

"Captain O'Shaughnessy makes a compelling case that pilots' psychological well-being can be, and should be, enhanced to catapult aviation safety to new heights."

— Colleen Hensely,
USAF pilot, airline pilot, leadership author, and speaker

"Captain O'Shaughnessy has provided us with a glimpse inside the cockpit that will enhance air safety for the betterment of all—now and in the future. The insight that she brings regarding mental health in aviation is long overdue. Bravo!"

— Christina Frederick, PhD,
professor of Department of Human Factors and Behavioral Neurobiology,
Embry-Riddle University

"Reyné O'Shaughnessy's book, *This Is Your Captain Speaking*, is an important contribution to the discussion surrounding the urgent problem of pilot mental health. I highly recommend this book for the aviator, the policy maker, and the curious."

— William Hoffman, MD, FAA AME,
aeromedical researcher, Georgetown University,
author of *Wings of Deceit: One Secret that Changes Everything* and
Intrepid Pursuit: When Stopping Is Not an Option

This Is Your Captain Speaking

What You Should Know About Your Pilot's Mental Health

Captain Reyné O'Shaughnessy

Published in the United States by
Ignite Press
5070 N. Sixth St. #189
Fresno, CA 93710
www.IgnitePress.us

ISBN: 979-8-9850682-0-7
ISBN: 979-8-9850682-1-4 (eBook)

For bulk purchase and for booking, contact:

Reyné O'Shaughnessy
CaptainReyneO.com

Library of Congress Control Number: 2021911535

Cover design by Teguh Kanseristia
Edited by Emma Hatcher
Interior design by Eswari Kamireddy

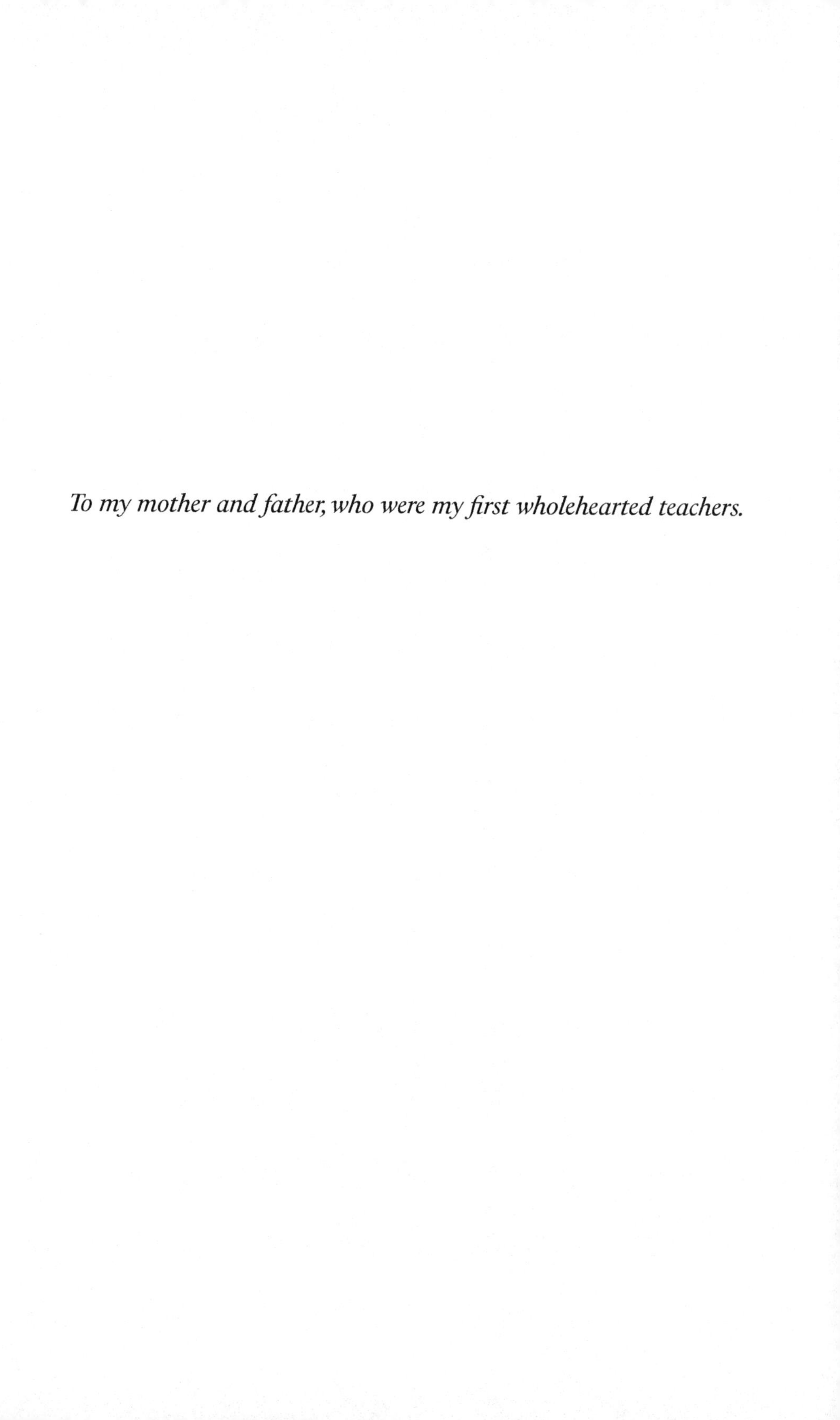

To my mother and father, who were my first wholehearted teachers.

ACKNOWLEDGEMENTS

To each and every one who has inspired me to be their voice.

CONTENTS

FOREWORD

The magic of aviation is woven deep into the fabric of American society. From the pioneering days of the Wright Flyer to the awe-inspiring future of commercial space travel, aviation has roused the sense of adventurism in millions while bringing the world closer together. At the heart of aviation, of course, is the aviator and the experiences that they carry with them. But along with their knowledge and skill, there is something else that pilots bring that too often remains unspoken.

Aviators are afraid to seek medical and psychological care because of what a new medical condition might mean to their future as a pilot. Even when they need it most, pilots too often avoid the medical or psychological system because of this concern, and it has direct consequences on their health. While knowledge of this trend is well known to both pilots and the aeromedical physicians who care for them, it is not well characterized in the medical literature. What this means is that one of the most significant problems facing modern aviation is not well understood and little is being done about it. In fact, not much has changed since this issue was identified over 100 years ago. Even the earliest pioneers in aerospace medicine knew that pilots would be leery of their doctors. Brigadier General (Dr.) Theodore Lyster of the US Army Air Corps published the first aerospace medicine textbook in the midst of World War I. He was an advocate for embedding physicians into flying units so that doctors could closely work with pilots and easily identify when something wasn't right. Today, the system has changed, but the same problems remain. The United States aeromedical system is based on pilot self-identification, and it often leaves a pilot having to decide whether to seek care and risk their career or continue to fly and risk their life.

Pilot healthcare aversion is wide reaching and expands across pilot demographics and medical conditions. Advocates are calling for change, and there seems to be reason to be hopeful. New policies have been enacted to address this barrier in select circumstances, but there is still so much work to be done. Our aeromedical research team feels strongly that quality data will be the cornerstone of any meaningful change, and we are working diligently to contribute to that aim.

Our studies are the largest ever published on pilot health seeking behavior and have finally quantified the prevalence of this phenomena.[1,2] Of 613 US pilots, 78.5% of pilots admitted to experiencing healthcare seeking anxiety due to their status as a pilot. This is at odds with the 28% of non-pilot controls who had similar feelings ($p = <0.001$). This trend remained true when we controlled for both age and gender, suggesting that being a pilot is a primary risk factor. There were 38.8% of pilots ($n=238$) who said that they had withheld information from a physician due to concern about their status as a pilot and 60.2% of pilots ($n=369$) who said that they had withheld or delayed seeking care for the same reason. With approximately 633,000 pilots in the United States, it is easy to see the broad implications to these numbers. While I'm sure these statistics are not surprising to pilots and their doctors, these are some of the first ever published. We are energized by the great deal of research going on with our partners in industry, academia, and government to better understand this important problem.

In addition to the many other conditions that take pilots out of the cockpit and impact their health, mental health has taken a forefront in the aviation community. Several large studies have demonstrated that conditions like major depression and generalized anxiety disorder are more prevalent in pilots than even the general population.[3] In fact, emerging data suggests that being a pilot in and of itself is a risk factor for these conditions. Unfortunately, pilots are too often going without treatment because of what it may mean for their career and life. Beyond what it means to aviation safety, it is my belief that we in the aeromedical community have a responsibility to work toward addressing the barriers that pilots face when seeking medical care.

O'Shaughnessy's *This Is Your Captain Speaking: What You Should Know About Your Pilot's Mental Health* is an important contribution to the discussion surrounding pilot mental health and is a step forward in the conversation about what the future of aeromedical health should look like. Through more than thirty-five years of industry experience and tens of thousands of hours with pilots, she uses her unique perspective to help us understand the landscape we face in working for a better future.

While the future remains uncertain, I think there are reasons to be hopeful. Major change takes time, but it starts with a first step in the right direction. *This is Your Captain Speaking* is an important part of that step forward and is filled with wisdom to guide our path.

William R. Hoffman, MD, FAA AME
Physician, aeromedical researcher, and author of
Wings of Deceit: One Secret that Changes Everything and
Intrepid Pursuit: When Stopping Is Not an Option

PREFACE

Writing this book was more than a project to me: it was a labor of love. I have a unique and up-close perspective of mental health in the airline industry. Pilots struggle with mental health more than is realized by the public, regulators, and industry. The information in this book is what I've discovered through hundreds and hundreds of deeply rooted discussions with pilots—in and outside the cockpit, experts who deal strictly with aviation professionals, and my own experience with navigating mental health.

As a seasoned airline pilot for thirty-five years, I'm here to offer you some insight into the world of pilot mental health. I have seen and heard first-hand testimonials from pilots, air traffic controllers, and flight attendants who suffer from chronic stress, anxiety, and depression. Seemingly minor symptoms can contribute to, and most often do lead to, reduced concentration and awareness. This combination has the potential to undermine safety. Sadly, in my career spanning more than three decades, I have borne witness to the catastrophic consequences of ignoring these symptoms over time.

Some people resist seeking help with mental health issues because of societal stigma. Most people, if they so choose, may seek treatment and counseling with the freedom of knowing that doing so will not impact their career. However, for commercial pilots or air traffic controllers, this isn't the case. Seeking treatment can severely impact their careers due to the barriers in place by the legislation that governs pilot certification. If a pilot seeks treatment, or even engages in a conversation with their aeromedical examiner, it "tags" them to the regulatory apparatus pertaining to the medical certification that the Federal Aviation Administration (FAA) requires. This could lead to being grounded and possibly losing his or her livelihood. This dynamic does nothing more than drive the pilot underground in fear of being exposed and perhaps losing their livelihood.

Even though the current FAA federal regulations have improved somewhat over the past 20 years, it hasn't been enough for pilots to be honest when updating their twice a year medical required profile questionnaires. Since 2010, the FAA has been working with airlines and pilot unions with a goal of reducing the stigma and barriers of self-reporting mental health issues and improving treatment options. However, common conditions such as asthma, chronic stress, anxiety, depression, insomnia, and use and misuse of substance abuse go unreported among pilots, because the fear of potentially losing their job is greater than the struggle itself. Fear of grounding, generated within pilots, remains the greatest risk to flight safety with some not asking for help until it's too late. This needs change.

Public safety is at risk, and we need to do something about it. It's not a surprise that airlines don't want to talk about pilot mental health. Frankly, it would scare the hell out of the public! Would you want to place yourself or your family in the hands of a pilot who is struggling with the lack of mental health well-being—one that feels that they dare not seek treatment at the risk of losing their livelihood?

Mental health affects all of us, and thankfully, as a society, we have come a long way. However, we still have a long way to go. How ironic is it that many of the qualities that make us great pilots can be toxic to us as human beings. Through all of the layers of education, titles, and accomplishments, mental health well-being was never part of any school curriculum or recurrent training. We need to be taught how to take better care of our mental health similar to the way we take care of our physical health. There should be no difference. Science tells us there is more than just our neck that connects our mind and body.

At age fifty, I had a shocking discovery. I didn't know it at the time, but this pivotal moment would reshape the trajectory of my entire life. A routine checkup revealed catastrophically high blood pressure in the immanent stroke range. After twenty plus years of night flying so that I could be home during the day to be with my children, I had neglected to take care of myself. I was dedicated to my family and persevered in my personal and professional life. I wasn't listening to my body well, and it frequently meant ignoring signs of exhaustion, resulting in me becoming really vulnerable to a complete physical and mental breakdown. I didn't recognize that chronic stress was literally chipping away at my well-being. Being prescribed two drugs—hypertension medication for high blood pressure and Xanax - a drug for anxiety, neither of which I filled—was a giant wake-up call.

My journey toward healing included developing awareness of work-life balance and taking small, concrete actions to improve my mental and physical well-being. Shifting my mindset to listening to my body as an integrated, valued partner, worthy of time, care and compassion, has been a process. Shifting my mindset to learning techniques such as mindfulness meditation, better nutrition, improving sleep, and developing healthy new habits has radically increased the quality of my life both personally and professionally. I want to shout to the entire aviation community that, from what I have learned, they too can benefit through these life-transforming practices.

Change happens when people refuse to be silenced. I had to stand firm to what I know in my heart is true. I have been inspired to find my voice by hundreds of pilots and my volunteer work throughout my thirty-five years as a commercial airline pilot. Even though this book mainly focuses on pilots, the entire workforce, including ATC and flight attendants, must be mentally healthy to minimize risk. It has taken me quite a long time to develop my own voice, and now that I have it, I'm not going to be silent. I know what I have to say is of value and contributes to a step forward in the conversation about what the future of aeromedical health should look like. I'm constantly amazed at just how courageous and brave-speaking the truth is!

The time has come for government regulators, organizations, and individuals to take part in reforming FAA regulations surrounding mental health. It's a hopeful time. Pilots want freedom to seek treatment without barriers, without consequence to their livelihood. The methods employed to evaluate airline pilot psychological health need to be reviewed and renewed. Creating new policies, new programs, and a new platform that allow airline professionals the freedom to seek mental health issues without the threat to their livelihood could help mitigate potential threats to aviation safety.

Improving pilot mental health will improve public safety, leading to less risk and liability.

My experience of thirty-five years in the airline industry has taught me that it's no longer acceptable to only train pilots in technical skills and knowledge; a foundational component of well-being to support the technical training to sustain a high performance career in aviation is needed. Over the years, my understanding of what this means, and how we can build it, has been shaped by the hundreds of pilots, research, and aeromedical professionals that I've been fortunate to listen to and learn from.

What I present in this book is based on research regarding mental health, it's stigmas in the airline industry, and how this impacts the well-being of aviation professionals, airline organizations, and you, the public. I approached writing this book with a sense of nuance, because there are so many different factors to consider. It is not an exposé but rather an honest talk about topics that are long past due needing discussion and action.

PART I
PILOTS UNDERGROUND

ONE
AIR DISASTERS

The pilot of your airliner is perfectly trained and undergoes recurrent training every six to nine months. Without question, his or her pilot training is the best that money can buy—hands down, state-of-the-art. And we subconsciously think that pilots are different, somehow more mentally tough, because of their training, the selection process, and their experience. And there is some truth to that. But keep this in mind: Pilots work in a national and international regulated industry that has an admirable safety record, yet it is unforgiving. So, how is your pilot feeling? You ought to be asking the question, "Is a pilot's mental health a risk to aviation safety?"

Let's take a look beyond the technical proficiency training and airmanship skills to how pilots feel. We need to look in depth at the person behind the controls. Any chronic stress, anxiety, depression, insomnia, alcohol use or abuse, or suicidal thoughts.

Pilot mental health is not a popular subject. Pilots are a highly trained group of professionals known for their highly intellectual abilities and the ability to compartmentalize. Compartmentalizing is a means of disconnecting non-operational events of life from the thoughts necessary to safely operate an aircraft. Yet pilots are human and struggle like the rest of the general population. What's troublesome is that nobody is talking about what happens when these so-called *compartments* fill up and overflow into the pilot's professional life, their profession, which in turn can impact safety of flight.

This is our history:

- JetBlue Flight 191: In 2015, a JetBlue pilot was triggered into a panic attack brought on by mounting stress and anxiety. The airplane diverted into Amarillo, Texas.[4]
- American Airlines Flight 736: In 2016, a pilot was grounded at Detroit Metro Airport due to an excessive blood alcohol level.[4]
- Malaysia Flight 370: While we will never know all the details, it is believed that the pilot committed a mass-murder/suicide by crashing the airplane into the Indian Ocean.[4]
- Germanwings Flight 9525: A pilot flew an airplane into the French Alps, killing all 200 souls on board.[4]
- FedEx Flight 705: An off-duty pilot tried to hijack the airplane shortly after takeoff with the intent to crash the airplane so his family could receive his life insurance policy.[4]
- Delta Flight 1728: A pilot who was scheduled to fly from Minneapolis-Saint Paul International Airport to San Diego International Airport was arrested prior to the flight for intoxication.[4]
- JetBlue Flight 584: A pilot flew an aircraft from John F. Kennedy International Airport to Orlando International Airport and back while legally drunk with a 0.11 blood alcohol level.[4]
- JetBlue Flight 1052: A flight attendant announced over the PA that he had been abused by a passenger, then grabbed and consumed two beers.[4]

Those are just a few big story headlines. The truth is that there are more stories of distress on board aircraft that don't hit the news. Even before the pandemic, pilots wouldn't disclose a mental health issue to their aeromedical examiner (AME) because of the stigma and fear of losing their license and perhaps losing their income. In 2020, there was a significant uptick in stressors, including the beginning of the COVID-19 pandemic. The pandemic crisis has exposed flight crews, their relatives, and passengers to particularly high psychological stressors. A few worth mentioning are:

- Increased workload due to intensive operations, emergency operations, or crisis situations in flight operations.
- Changed cooperation and team climate due to preventative measures.
- Increased risk of infection due to contact with potentially infected workers, passengers, and surfaces at the airport, on the flight deck, and in the cabin.
- Additional workflows and work processes by handling infected passengers or crew.
- Long and irregular working hours, reduced rest opportunities, and potential fatigue, combined with difficult situations at home.
- Home quarantine for those infected or exposed to the virus.
- Job insecurity, loss of income, and potential loss of employment for some.

These stressors can lead to psychological strains, which can negatively affect a crew member's ability to safely perform their jobs.

I'm not saying that all pilots have a diagnosable mental illness or substance addiction. What I am saying is that everyone has a right to access resources to help them if needed *without barriers, without potential risk to their career.* All of us have a mind that needs to be cared for in the same way that we take care of our physical well-being.

Stress, anxiety, and depression are a few commonly occurring mental health concerns. Don't get me wrong—stress is a part of our culture. We can't eliminate it. Research indicates that a considerable portion of the United States population suffers from some form of mental health issue that leads to emotional unfitness that takes us off the day-to-day spectrum of stress adjustments. Most go undiagnosed and untreated. A similar rate of occurrence appears to be found within the airline pilot population. The stigma surrounding mental health, coupled with current legislation could lead a pilot to losing his or her livelihood if a mental health concern is revealed, leads pilots underground and leaves them shunning treatment. One would argue that, looking at the evidence, it is better to have a policy that allows pilots to use medication and continue to operate with appropriate medical supervision and precautions than to have a policy that ground pilots when they are prescribed medication other than the four antidepressants approved by legislation as this rigidity may result in pilots flying when depressed and with untreated mental health conditions. Confessing too much on a physical exam questionnaire can be risky, and it can unnecessarily disqualify a pilot.

Pilots and air traffic controllers have the tremendous responsibility of ensuring safety at all costs. After a long and satisfying career as an airline pilot, my role now is safety advocate for the public, individual, and aviation organizational interests. I've seen how seemingly minor symptoms of burnout, stress, anxiety, and depression have contributed to reduced awareness and concentration that can lead to an undermining of safety in the skies, to say nothing of the effect on the individuals involved.

Since 1994, there have been at least six suspected or confirmed passenger airplane crashes caused by the intentional action of a pilot. Those apparent suicides resulted in a total of 398 fatalities, according to the US Department of Health. The International Civil Aviation

Organization reported more than 100 commercial aircraft accidents as of 2019.

I read everything that I can get my hands on pertaining to airline safety. I don't have to dig too deep to find publications and articles regarding unsafe or even deadly actions by pilots suffering from mental health challenges. A 2018 article that appeared in the *International Journal of Aviation Aeronautical and Aerospace* crossed my desk.[8] It discussed the perils of ignoring possible mental health challenges that might undermine aviation safety. Some were life-threatening events; other incidents, while not posing an immediate lethal threat to passenger or crew safety, compromised safe operations.

Science-based evidence proves that more than just our neck connects our head and our body. There is no body-mind separation in our health.

The good news is that we've come a long way from mid-twentieth century stigmas, when mental health was considered taboo. A problem that our country shouldn't tolerate in an age of great abundance, resources and technological progress.

Science-based evidence proves that more than just our neck connects our head and our body. There is no body-mind separation in our health.

TWO
A DEEPER LOOK

As a number of authors, such as Kalkman, have demonstrated, there is a strong evidence base linking air accidents to poor mental health amongst pilots. Let's take a deeper look at some of the aviation events involving mental health issues mentioned in the previous chapter. The following stories have been recorded in aviation history and are remembered with unspeakable sadness. Even though not all of the disasters are the same, they all have one thing in common—tragedy that stemmed from untreated or mistreated mental health issues.

- **JetBlue Flight 191 Airbus 320**—On March 27, 2012, JetBlue Flight 191 was operating from New York's John F. Kennedy Airport to Las Vegas. The plane diverted to Amarillo following disturbing comments and threats made by the aircraft's captain. Recognizing the captain's bizarre behavior, the aircraft's first officer arranged for the captain to go out of the cockpit to check on something. When he left the cockpit, the first officer locked him out of the flight deck. In the cabin, passengers subdued the captain. An off-duty JetBlue pilot assisted the first officer in the uneventful diversion to Amarillo. The initial reports by the company said the captain suffered from a panic attack, though mental health professionals suggest that something more complicated likely contributed to his behavior.[4]

- **Malaysia Flight 370 Boeing** 777—In March 2014, Malaysia Flight 370 operating from Kuala Lumpur, Malaysia, to Beijing disappeared over the Indian Ocean. Twelve crew members and 227 passengers were lost. The unsuccessful search for the aircraft continued until the Australian Transport Safety Board regulators terminated it in January 2017 after more than 1,000 days. The search was handicapped by the failure or possible disabling of the automatic aircraft reporting systems—the aircraft's transponder and reporting system. After the first thirty-eight minutes of flight, nothing was heard from the aircraft again.[4]

The small amounts of wreckage that were recovered led investigators to suspect that the aircraft was not configured for a water landing or ditching when it ultimately plunged into the ocean. In fact, the aircraft was not configured in a manner conducive to crew and passenger survival. As a result, investigators concluded that someone was controlling the aircraft at the end of its flight. Investigators found the captain's personal computer at his home indicating that he had made computer-simulated flights in a Boeing 777-200LR, piloting the aircraft into remote areas of the Indian Ocean. The revelation of aircraft configuration and the captain's simulated flights led some investigators to believe that the disappearance of the plane was a calculated suicide / mass murder carried out by the captain. Ultimately, however, the Australian Transport Safety Bureau concluded that the reason for the crash couldn't be determined with certainty as long as the primary body of wreckage remains undiscovered.[4]

- **Germanwings Flight 9525 Airbus 320**—On March 24, 2015, Germanwings Flight 9525 was operating from Barcelona, Spain, to Düsseldorf, Germany, when it crashed in the Alps killing all 150 passengers and crew. Reports indicate that the aircraft leveled off at 38,000 feet as the flight crew turned the aircraft toward a point on their flight plan in the French Alps. Up until this point, nothing was out of order. There was a routine conversation in which the flight crew, joined by a flight attendant, discussed the turnaround in Barcelona and their late departure. The captain then left the flight deck to use the lavatory, leaving the first officer in control of the aircraft. Alone on the flight deck, the first officer chose an altitude of 100 feet on the autopilot altitude selector and retarded the auto throttles to flight idle, which caused the autopilot to pitch the aircraft downward to maintain airspeed.[4]

Despite efforts by the captain, cabin crew, and air traffic control to reach the first officer via radio and the flight deck door communicator, the aircraft continued its descent, hitting the ground at nearly 350 knots—525 mph, killing all onboard. As investigators begin to unravel the events before the crash, a disturbing revelation is uncovered. The first officer, who had been flying for Germanwings for less than one year, had ongoing mental health issues since 2009. In fact, since 2009, his medical certificate, renewed annually, included a waiver for a severe depressive episode without psychotic symptoms. In December, roughly four months prior to the crash, the pilot's depression returned. He sought treatment from several mental health professionals and was given multiple authorizations from doctors that permitted him to take time off from his flight duties. Not all of these authorizations were forwarded to Germanwings, nor did the first officer disclose to his employer or aviation

> medical examiner that his depression had returned. The accident unleashed a torrent of activity as aviation regulatory agencies around the world sought to better understand the implications of mental health on the flight deck.[4]

The FAA requires every airline transport pilot to obtain a Class I Medical Certificate every six months.[4] Each year, the FAA processes approximately 450,000 applications for Class I, II, and III medical certificates.[4] Class II medicals are required for commercial pilots, and Class III for student, recreational, and private pilots.[4] Applications are completed online, and then the pilot visits an FAA-designated Aviation Medical Examiner (AME).[4] This qualified aeromedical physician evaluates the physical and mental well-being of the pilot.[4] A Class I medical exam is typically administered for commercial airlines pilots every six months. It is a key part of a pilot's privileges to operate an airline transport aircraft. Without it a pilot is grounded indefinitely.

> The problem is, unless the pilot self-reports a lack of their emotional fitness to their aeromedical physician, it goes undetected.

Prior to the pilot's first class medical appointment with an aviation medical examiner, the pilot completes an extensive medical questionnaire (FAA- Form 8500-9). The physical examination is the most thorough and includes blood pressure, heart function, and heart valves, electrocardiograms, a vision test, and urine analysis.

Item 18 - medical history - asks the pilot to self-report any of the following: substance dependency, alcohol dependency, or suicidal thoughts. If the pilot answers the questions truthfully, it results in automatic grounding. If the pilot answers a question untruthfully and is later discovered, it is grounds for the airmanship license to be revoked. Therein lies the problem - damned if you do, damned if you don't. As the career for many airline pilots has become more stressful due to a wide variety of factors, psychological illness and burnout is becoming more prevalent as it goes unreported.

The problem is, unless the pilot self-reports a lack of their emotional fitness to their aeromedical physician, the condition goes undetected. The barriers and consequences of the current legislation force pilots to go underground, potentially to self-medicate or to not medicate at all, either of which can be dangerous.

If a pilot is honest about their struggles with stress, anxiety, depression, insomnia, and alcohol use and abuse with a medical examiner, the AME does have some discretion, however, as mandated by their medical license, the AME is required to report it to the FAA. Now, a big, fat, shining light is cast upon the pilot. What would it take for pilots to feel free to discuss their mental health struggles without creating an avenue of problems for themselves? One thing is for sure: current legislation barriers need to come down for a pilot before he or she would feel completely protected to self-report.

THREE
TRUTH UNDER PRESSURE

Becoming a professional airline pilot is a coveted and prestigious position. It requires mental and physical fortitude as well as a tough mentality. Pilots are seen as superhuman for a variety of reasons that date back to the beginning of military aviation where the pride that has always been a part of the profession was used against pilots. Today, the threat of losing the associate professional and social status still has a great impact on pilots, as often seen after an unsuccessful training or mandatory checking events. With that in mind, pilots are human beings and are no different from other humans. We struggle, and we suffer.

It's no secret that being a commercial airline pilot is a stressful career for a variety of reasons. It is considered the second most dangerous profession, as reported by *Industrial Safety Hygiene News* in November 2020, and the third most stressful job, according to *Business Daily News* in November 2019. These factors included in this report are physical demands, on-the-job hazards, environmental conditions, and the risk of personal injury or injury to another for whom the worker is directly responsible.

A 2018 front-page poll in the *USA Today* listed airline pilots as the third most stressful profession behind active-duty military personnel and first responders. Another recent large-scale study revealed 13% of pilots met the criteria for depression and 4.1% considered suicide in the previous two weeks. Think about that: If an airline has 5,000 crewmembers, there are 675 of them that can be qualified as being depressed, and between two and five of them would potentially fall inside a potential-suicide category. It's no wonder that the airline industry doesn't want to talk about this issue. It would frighten the flying public.

I sure as hell don't want to be perceived as weak, and neither do any of my colleagues who think that they have The Right Stuff! Pilots are reluctant to talk about issues such as stress, anxiety, depression, insomnia, and behaviors such as alcohol use or abuse, or concerns about personal performance.

None of us are eager to disclose deeply personal information. Pilots believe that being vulnerable, sharing feelings or emotions would be, at best, humiliating or embarrassing and, at worst, the end of their flying career. They keep quiet, go underground, and put off doing anything about it until they can hardly function as a crewmember anymore and are forced to take action.

The mental health problems of pilots who eventually go out on medical leave don't develop overnight. Most handle it fine, right up until the time that they don't. They suffer, sometimes for years. Most pilots delay in getting help because the idea of self-disclosure seems even scarier than the anxiety they are living with. Diagnosing psychological maladies is not the result of a definitive and immediate discovery. It is more of a long-term analysis with an apparent discovery. To the flying public, this is not the best news. However, not every pilot has a diagnosable mental illness. Many are manageable. Many don't consider that there are others like them who are also struggling, and currently, there isn't a platform in place that pilots 120% trust to seek resources and refuge.

Many pilots go out on medical leave when they perceive reaching the point of no other options. As opposed to admitting anxiety or depression, a pilot may claim something they feel safer about disclosing—back pain is a pretty common way out. Use your imagination! It is only a fraction of pilots who actually decide to tell the truth, usually as forced disclosure after an incident or an accident event. Their carefully guarded secret comes out—to their family, union, company, physician(s), and the FAA—the 800-pound gorilla in the room.

In addition to the medical certificate being essential to a pilot keeping their job, neither the traditionally macho aviation culture, nor the world of corporate airlines are friendly to humanistic self-reflection. While many business entities worldwide have begun or are beginning to embrace partnering with employees about mental health awareness, airlines offer little or no preventative wellbeing and good health programs to raise such awareness specifically tailored for their pilots. The role of a pilot is unique, and it requires unique education on how to take care of their mental health. From navigating home life to inherited pressures of the job such as commuting, lack of nutrition on the road, dehydration, time zones, layovers in different cities/hotels every night, irregular work hours, sitting for long periods of time in an aircraft, dry air in a cockpit, excessive noise in cockpit, lack of oxygen at high altitudes, exposure to solar and cosmic radiation, added security checks at airports, disruptive sleeping patterns, limited fitness access, and flying from coast to coast (or around the world) are a few work-related components that induce burnout, stress, anxiety, and depression, and we know with certainty that, over time, these hindrances compound.

Currently, to address stressors and self-imposed behaviors such as stress, substance use, and abuse by pilots, airline unions have developed in-house, peer-to-peer committees to help mitigate biological, psychological, and social behaviors. Stressors can be internal or external events that happen in a person's life, such as a finances, teens, naughty teens, elderly parents, purchasing a new house, divorce, or a death in the family, or they might be job-related events, such as unpredictable schedule, failed check rides, failed training events, conflict with colleagues, an event in the flight, or a furlough. The intent of these committees is to utilize volunteer pilots to help peers cope. These committee's encourage pilots to call in to a central number if they are experiencing stressors on the road or at home, and a peer will be assigned to them. These conversations are not reportable to either the airline or the FAA.

This is a good time to disclose that I was one of the peer-to-peer volunteers at my airline and to dive deeper into understanding the role of volunteer pilots who staff these committees. I like to call them fellow travelers. As well intended as the pilots are who make up these committees, these committees are, at best, a resource center. Here's how it works: The pilot volunteer is alerted through a phone system that a fellow pilot is in need of help. He or she is assigned and, within a day, reaches out to the instressed pilot. The volunteer listens to the pilot and offers resources best fitted to the pilot's needs. Here's something interesting. Although the "fellow travelers" programs that are in place have value for minor troubles, most pilots don't utilize them until they hit a brick wall. In which case, the struggling pilot is beyond friendly phone calls. At this point he or she needs professional intervention. And even though a pilot may be aware that confidential help is available and encouraged by their airline and union, they don't go. Why? They feel handcuffed by the current legislation pertaining to pilot mental health. Fear of disclosure to his or her aeromedical physician and mistrust of their union and company contribute to the reasons pilots go underground. Concern over stigma and the desire to remain employed are two very powerful motivators, and two very good reasons to avoid detection. It's a global concern.

The regulatory agencies in the United States have surely perpetuated, albeit not intentionally, a culture of dishonesty in pilots. However, in 2015, the FAA started to work with airlines and pilot unions to better understand the area of mental health and its symptoms to help reduce the stigma of self-reporting while improving treatment options.[4] Currently, the FAA regulations tied to mental health appear reasonable and well thought out; but, in reality, pilots view them as useless and outdated.[4] Even though the industry has evolved somewhat, it has yet to come up with systemic solutions that encourage pilots to self-report free of barriers or consequences.

FOUR
NO MORE WHISPERS

Globally, roughly 264 million people suffer from depression.[5] While effective treatments exist, fewer than half of those with depression around the world receive treatment, according to the World Health Organization.[5] Pilots are no different than the general population. In the past five years (2016–2021) pilot mental health has begun to get the attention that it deserves, giving me more motivation to write this book.[5] Here are a few things that you should know about your pilot's mental health.

A code of silence surrounds mental health issues in the cockpit. In 2016, Harvard conducted a study concerning pilot mental health. According to an anonymous survey of nearly 1,850 pilots at the Harvard T. H. Chan School of Public Health, it was discovered that hundreds of commercial airline pilots currently flying might be clinically depressed. The study highlighted the prevalence of depression among pilots—a group of professionals who are responsible every day for thousands of lives and operating hundreds of millions of pieces of equipment worth hundreds of millions of dollars that can cause a neighbor's mass destruction.[6]

The Harvard study was the first to examine airline pilot mental health with a focus on depression and suicidal thoughts. The information was gathered outside of the information derived from aircraft accident investigations, regulated health examinations, or identifiable self-reports, all of which are records protected by civilian aviation authorities and airline companies.[6]

According to the study authors, there is a strong disincentive for pilots to self-report if they are suffering from depressive symptoms. Joseph Allen, assistant professor of exposure assessment science and senior author of the study said, "It may be that they are not seeking treatment due to the fear of negative career impacts."[6]

The study findings underscore the importance of accurately assessing pilots' mental health and increasing support for preventive treatment. The findings from the Harvard study were published in *Environmental Health* magazine in December 2016, approximately one and a half years after a Germanwings tragedy.[6]

Respondents to the web-based survey, conducted between April and December 2015, came from over fifty countries. The survey's standardized questions about job content and health were drawn from the Job Content Questionnaire and the US Centers for Disease Control and Prevention's National Health and Nutrition Examination Survey. It included questions about mental health that doctors use to diagnose depression. The survey was designed with a variety of questions so as not to suggest a focus on mental health, in order to minimize potential bias in responses.[6]

The highest percentage of respondents initiated surveys from the United States (45.5%), Canada (12.6%), and Australia (11.1%). Out of nearly 3,500 who participated in the survey, 1,848 completed the questions about mental health. Within this group, 233 (12.6%) met the criteria for likely depression, and seventy-five (4.1%) reported having suicidal thoughts within the previous two weeks. Of 1,430 who reported working as an airline pilot in the last seven days at the time of the survey, 193 (13.5%) met the criteria for depression.

Female pilots were more likely than male pilots to have at least one day of poor mental health during the previous month, and were more likely to have been diagnosed with depression. The study also found that depression was more likely among pilots who used higher levels of sleep aid medication and those who were experiencing sexual harassment. A greater proportion of male pilots than female pilots reported that they had experiences nearly every day of loss of interest, feeling like a failure, trouble concentrating, and thinking that they would be better off dead.[7]

In May 2021, I had the privilege of interviewing Dr. William Hoffman, a physician, FAA aeromedical examiner, and aeromedical researcher in San Antonio who has been published in the United States as well as international medical journals. Dr. Hoffman and his team know well the problem that pilots face when seeking medical care. In partnership with Georgetown University School of Medicine and several other institutions, their aim is to generate quality data to identify specific interventions that could be identified and proposed to decrease the barriers that pilots face when deciding whether to seek medical and psychological care.

Dr. Hoffman shared with me that there is a research project under the direction of his team that is expected to be published by the end of 2021. This project studies the history and healthcare-seeking behavior of more than 4,000 pilots in the United States. In the survey, pilots are asked about their history of healthcare (medically and psychologically) and their choice of non-aeromedical providers with the hope of understanding where pilots choose to seek practitioners for potential treatment. If a clear trend were identified (i.e., chiropractor, dentist office, internet, etc.), then interventions could be targeted to that potential outlet.

Pilots are also asked in the survey about the history of symptoms (both physical and psychological) experienced before flying and how that impacted their go/no-go decision and pre-flight safety assessment. In this study, such an intervention could assist pilots in pre-flight safety assessments as it relates to health. While this may not be the single key to solving this major issue, it is the first ever prospective research on interventions to address pilot specific healthcare barriers.

This is the largest study ever conducted that targets pilot healthcare-seeking behavior, and it will likely be a major tool in the path forward. However, this is what is most exciting—this study has received broad support from the aviation community and been shared by several large United States airlines, the Civil Air Patrol, the United States Air Force, and multiple other organizations. "Beyond the research, we are working to develop relationships with key policy makers and organizations," Dr. Hoffman said. "When the data finally is available, we want to make sure it gets in the hands of the right people to impact change."

In addition to Dr. Hoffman and his team studying pilot healthcare-seeking behavior, they are partnering with several other organizations to build a better understanding of this trend. They have recently started work with the Department of Aerospace at the University of North Dakota and several other federal agencies to continue on both descriptive epidemiological and prospective case-control studies.

Hoffman is also collaborating with Canadian researchers at the University of Alberta to better understand similar issues that pilots around the world face. "This is an international problem and we need to look in all settings for solutions," said Hoffman.

Interestingly enough, while my book was in the publication process, I reached out to the University of Alberta Canada to find out more about their work. Their survey, similar to Dr. Hoffman's, asked pilots to fill out a de-identified survey about the impact that preserving an aviation flight medical certificate might have on a pilot's overall health.

The designers of the Canadian survey's intent was to determine how pilots perceive aeromedical care and whether the risk of losing their license due to medical complications inhibits the seeking of medical and psychological advice. In the United States, pilots still have to self-report to the FAA the truth about the state of their health—physically and psychologically. "Pilots may be receiving less than the standard of care because they aren't able to openly share pertinent medical information," the survey authors said.[7]

And if that wasn't enough, an article was published in the EU Guardian (June 2021) titled "Warning Over Pilots' Mental Health as Planes Return to the Skies."[32] The authors of this article explain airlines are overlooking the mental health and well-being of pilots and other aviation workers in their scramble to get planes flying again, according to researchers. Many aviation workers experienced anxiety, stress, and depression during COVID-19 lockdowns, but they report feeling discouraged from acknowledging problems or seeking help, creating potential safety hazards and health problems.[7,8]

The warning came from the *Lived Experience and Wellbeing Project*—a Trinity College Dublin hub that studies aviation worker well-being and its impact on performance and flight safety—as airlines across the world increase flights and start rehiring pilots and crew.

"We can't sweep this under the carpet or dress it up. The data says a certain number of pilots were struggling pre-COVID but they wouldn't disclose a mental health issue to their employer because of the stigma and fear of losing their license and perhaps losing their salary. Just as airlines have procedures to ensure that mothballed planes are airworthy, humans need attention too, said Paul Cullen, a Human Factors researcher. You need to do the same for the crew to make sure they're airworthy."[8]

The team conducted a survey of more than 1,000 pilots worldwide in 2019 and found that 18% had moderate depression and 80% had moderate burnout. More than three-quarters of the respondents said that they would not disclose such issues to employers and 81% said that they did not feel valued by employers.[8]

A second survey of more than 2,000 aviation workers, mostly pilots, cabin crew, air traffic controllers—in August 2020 found they suffered more than the general population during the pandemic. A fifth of pilots and 58% of cabin crew reported moderate depression, compared with 23% for the Irish and UK populations as a whole.[8]

It was reported that many aviation workers lost incomes during the pandemic, and some experienced having their home or car repossessed. Once back at work, those workplace hazards that were an issue pre-COVID will come back, but the individuals' resilience won't be as strong as before, and this reality could potentially impact on flight safety.[8]

After the pilot Andreas Lubitz deliberately crashed the Germanwings plane in 2015, killing all 150 people onboard, the European Commission ordered airlines to assess pilots psychologically before recruitment. The rules seek to prevent a similar tragedy by offering pilots access to a support program in case of mental health problems.[8]

The industry, however, does not gather data on well-being, and some pilots fear reporting mental health problems or accepting help (for instance, peer-support programs), they could lose their license to fly, said Joan Cahill, the Trinity team's principal investigator.[8]

Well-being is a factor in safe performance, and employers need to do **more** than offer access to gyms and yoga, said Joan Cahill. "They need to provide support for their staff—mental health awareness training. The regulations are not for forcing airlines to do this, and it's driving pilots with well-being issues underground."[8]

Flexible rosters and crew-pairing processes, along with practices to encourage openness, can protect crew well-being and airline safety, she said. "Given current licensing requirements and cultural norms, aviation workers are unlikely to acknowledge problems and seek support/

help. When somebody is ill, we want them to put their hand up and acknowledge this and seek help."[8]

Niven Phoenix, a commercial pilot who heads Kura Human Factors, a company that trains pilots and advises airlines, said that some were "willfully blind" to the topic of well-being because it was inconvenient.[8]

"There is a whole host of evidence out there that organizations don't want to listen to. Aviation is very, very safe, but it is so unforgiving."[8] More focus on staff well-being would protect licenses, livelihoods, and *lives*. Awareness is the key to change.

Janet Northcote, a spokesperson for the European Union Aviation Safety Agency (EASA), said that the industry and regulators worked with aviation psychology representatives and other specialists to enhance workers' well-being and help them cope with any "well-being degradation" before it became a safety hazard.[8]

Peer-support groups, training, and awareness activities take place regularly across Europe, and the agency had flagged the potential degradation of skills during the 2020–2021 pandemic as part of a Return to Normal Operations project, said Northcote.[8]

"It has also focused on the impact of COVID-related events (isolation, losing loved ones, being unwell yourself, or having sick relatives) on the well-being of crew members, and suggested ways to mitigate these potential hazards."[8]

I felt that it was important to bring to my readers' attention this current research regarding pilot mental health attitudes from all around the world. This research speaks to the growing awareness and critical nature of this topic and is in exact alignment with the focus of this book. To counter the effects of biological, psychological, and psychosocial stressors on pilots' mental health and to mitigate its impact on flight safety, it is clear that more preventive measures are needed and that the current legislation in the United States needs change and airlines need to implement wellbeing and good health education through pilot's recurrent training cycles. When it comes to education regarding mental health for pilots, we must be proactive rather than reactive.

FIVE
GIVING VOICE

A fellow colleague of mine took his life one afternoon when his wife stepped out to the grocery store. Harry's untimely death devastated all of us—his children, family, coworkers, and friends. After the discovery of the Harvard study, coupled with the sadness of Harry's untimely death, I knew that I couldn't keep quiet any longer. For thirty-five years, I have listened to broken stories, and it is time to give voice to the voiceless, to cultivate inner courage, and to speak the truth, even under pressure.

Over the past three years, I've interviewed more than 100 pilots from around the world. Although I can't share every story with you, I've chosen several stories that represent situations that most of us can relate to. Why is storytelling important? Stories help us personalize facts and put a human experience to the details presented. It helps us understand why things happen in the ways that they do. The meaning that other people create from telling their stories can help us live differently. We tell ourselves stories about our world all day long. Our stories are particularly important when they define our sense of identity, such as the career we've chosen or the people we love. So, I'm curious. Is there a story that is a core story of who you are? Is there a story you tell yourself that impacts your relationships and well-being?

Other people's stories help us reappraise our own. We can learn through vicarious or fictitious experiences. Authentic stories are rooted in vulnerability. They are from scars, not active wounds, and reflect the meaning pulled from experiences. The following stories were powerful for me to hear. They resonated for many reasons, mostly because I could be their sister, wife, mother, or their friend. The time in the pilots' lives during which these stories took place was not easy. But I don't think that they'd be where they are today without these experiences. The search for significance in their experiences makes these stories deeply core to their sense of identity. Names have been changed to protect the privacy of the pilots. I hope that you read these accounts with interest, compassion, and empathy, knowing that one day these scenarios could reflect you or someone that you care about.

Falling to Pieces
Luis, Boeing 767 Captain

Depression can be triggered by memories. In Luis's case, they haunted him. Like a house built on top of a graveyard, no matter how happy and uneventful life was on the surface, there was that feeling that he would never be able to walk away from the cobwebs of his memories. His life felt like a patchwork of incomplete and traumatic stories with many secrets in between that never allowed them to fully connect. All of it was glued together by actual happy moments that would somewhat let the dark moments tuck away in an unreachable part of his brain. It accumulated into a deep and distant hard drive that would eventually run out of space and begin to mess with the operating system that he used to live his life.

The secret and lies were the most haunting, for they always left an incomplete sense of who he was, flooding his mind with *whys* and somehow making him feel responsible for all the emotional pain that had transpired in his past. Luis's passions of family, nature, and soaring would keep those memories stored in check. Like most Type A personality types, achievement became a driving force in his life with the unconscious belief that somehow—if "he made it"—when "he arrived," the pain would all fade away. But it did not.

As life went on, his emotions continued piling up with more traumatic events added onto the hard drive. His family business in Argentina failed and was taken away. The unspeakably sad event of September 11, 2001, directly impacted the fleet where he was an instructor. Together with his company filing for bankruptcy, SARS, and a marriage stressor of infertility, everything continued to pile up. But Luis kept it all compartmentalized.

Then, his daughter Victoria arrived in 2004. After twelve years of trying, the missing piece in their marriage blessed Luis and his wife Marilyn. The gift of their daughter would bring back the joy missing in his marriage. Or so he thought.

A year-and-a-half after Victoria was born, Marilyn was in the hospital with symptoms of heart attack. After a full day of tests, she was diagnosed with chronic fatigue, severe anxiety, and untreated postpartum depression. They decided to seek a second opinion. In some ways, the diagnosis seemed unbelievable yet, on the other hand, totally understandable. The psychologist/psychiatrist agreed with the diagnosis and recommended that Marilyn begin taking medications. Luis was blown away when the doctor turned to him and said, "and you too!"

In Luis's case, his depression was a buildup of life events that held him hostage in his own mind. Some describe depression as a lake that obscures repressed memories on its muddy bottom, invisible beneath the surface. Treatment is described as discovering what lies at the depths of the lake. This metaphor is symbolic of repressed memories, emotions, and pain, but here's the tricky part—you don't know all those things when you first get diagnosed.

"I had no idea that my compartmentalized muddy pond was full and had overflowed with deep dark emotions and memories. Here's how my story begins: it began long before I was born, but is an example of what, how, and why depression compounds through a lifetime."

Luis did not recognize he was absorbing Marilyn's pain and had spiraled into a depression of his own. This happens when a person is so sensitive to emotions that they absorb negativity. When their psychologist/psychiatrist diagnosed and prescribed medication for both of them, the first thought that crossed his mind was to ask her, "How did you know?" Luis had felt this heaviness but couldn't identify it.

"I had no idea that my compartmentalized muddy pond was full and had overflowed with deep dark emotions and memories. Here's how my story begins: it began long before I was born, but is an example of what, how, and why depression compounds through a lifetime."

"I didn't feel "me," I just couldn't feel well. Nothing I did seemed to bring any joy; joy was an elusive concept that everyone could have except me. I remember one night flipping through channels on the television and every channel felt like a wagon of a train full of wonderful lives that I couldn't have."

He began quietly reaching out to resources. He ended up seeing a cognitive behavioral therapist (CBT) before starting the medication. Additionally, the therapist recommended the book, *Feeling Good: The New Mood Therapy* (by David Burns). The whole process was an incredible learning experience. Their therapist in the United States recommended a psychologist for Luis and a psychiatrist for Marilyn (since she was taking medication) in Argentina. They were a couple and happy to work with another couple.

Both were professors at the local university and therapy began to feel more like an incredible process of learning how their own brain functioned. It was amazing how they were taught so many things in school, but not how their brains work and how to relate to others, which they confessed is the most important aspect of their lives. Through therapy (mainly CBT), Luis learned about the many cognitive distortions that were driving his lack of emotional well-being.

"Friends asked me, 'What is it like to go through therapy for depression? And I would say, It's like going through open brain surgery without anesthesia. It's painful. However, it was also immensely insightful and powerful. Up to that point, I would say I felt like I had been flying my life in raw data, and now, I am being introduced to the Flight Management System of my brain. I could see how a lot of my painful memories had been transformed into subroutines that would keep me in the hole. Cognitive therapists called these 'cognitive distortions.' Feeling responsible for all that I had experienced as a child and feeling responsible for my wife's happiness were just two of those distortions."

During his last weeks of therapy, the chronic back pain Luis had experienced for years increased significantly and he began to get cramps in his left leg. Luis's friend and massage therapist suspected that the issue could be more than just muscle tightness related to stress. He eventually followed her advice and made an appointment with his doctor. An MRI revealed a tumor the size of a tennis ball on Luis's sciatic nerve that required surgery.

Upon returning to the United States, Luis visited his doctor. The good news was that he had received a letter from his psychologist stating he was cleared to return back to work. The bad news was the tumor that required weeks of tests, a biopsy and a four-hour surgery. Luckily, the thirteen-centimeter schwannoma tumor was not cancerous. After a few intense weeks of rehab, he was ready to return to work. In all, his depression treatment and back surgery took five months.

Over the next four years though, Luis hit a turning point in his life. He shared that it was through a combination of cognitive based therapy (CBT), positive psychology, and mindfulness that his well-being started to thrive.

"Over the years, what I learned would bring a sense of normalcy to my world. Through mindfulness practice and finding my center, my well-being started to soar. I developed wonderful, magical, deep moments with my family. I spent mornings with my family and some afternoons paragliding. However, like many other things in life, I needed a tweak."

Luis's wife felt that he was spending too much time away flying and they argued about it a lot. These arguments sent Luis into a mental low. Paragliding had become a habit, something he loved doing and had become a part of who he was. He knew that he was spending too much time away from home and disconnecting too much. Paragliding had become one of the joys in Luis's life and, in hindsight, his addiction. Similar to most addictions, there's not a happy ending.

Luis decided to go one day to Boulder. Luis loved being out in nature and loved paragliding; the combination spoke to his soul. He flew from a low training site in North Boulder. A few other pilots and Luis were using the spot for advanced flying. Waiting for a thermal to rise up the slope, they would launch into it and let it carry them up thousands of feet.

This one time, Luis thought he missed the thermal. He was headed to the park below for landing when, suddenly, he saw a dust devil to the left, realizing that he had not missed the thermal after all. He headed straight for the dust devil to climb up and get in more flying. The moment he encountered it, he felt an incredible upward thrust and immediately realized he had made a fatal mistake. A paraglider does not have a frame like a hang glider, which makes flying into a dust devil prohibited at low altitudes. By the time that he realized his mistake, he saw that the wing was completely collapsing above his head and stalling. Luis was too low to effectively deploy his emergency parachute. He knew that he was about to die.

By instinct, he applied the stall recovery techniques. As he pulled down on the controls gently, he felt the jolt of the canopy re-opening above him like an umbrella that suddenly catches a gust of wind. The popping sound of the canopy inflating above him gave a moment to contemplate that perhaps, maybe, he might survive. Quickly, he realized that the canopy inflated into a "graveyard spiral"—one of the most difficult turns to recover from in a paraglider, especially with no altitude to accomplish it. When Luis saw the ground fast approaching, he yanked at the controls with no regards to a progressive recovery. The next thing Luis knew, he was looking at the blue sky like a little boy at the apex of the push in a swing, his back facing the ground below. He knew that the impact was coming next, and he knew that he would not survive the fall. Still tugging at the controls, he closed his eyes and awaited the fatal impact.

Luis hit the ground and felt the full brunt of the impact. When he opened his eyes, he found himself huddled in the fetal position in some weeds. He was alive, conscious and in excruciating agony. He recalled a motorcycle accident when he was seventeen and waited for the shock that would take the pain away. It never came. It felt as though his ribs had broken and penetrated his lungs. As he felt fluid accumulate in his lungs, he thought his destiny was sealed.

"Every breath felt like breathing into a dagger. I could not breathe any more. I rolled over onto my back looking at the sky; the weeds gently dancing in front of my eyes. I thought, 'This is it. This is how it all ends; the warm September breeze in my face, the weeds moving in the foreground, with the deep-blue sky in the background.'"

Luis spent two weeks in ICU in the trauma unit of Boulder Community Hospital, followed by two and half months at Craig Hospital in Denver, one of the few places in the US specializing in spinal cord injuries. The damage to his body was extensive—broken sternum, sacrum, coccyx, pelvis, two vertebrae, a collapsed lung, and a lacerated liver. His survival was doubtful.

The day after admittance to the trauma unit, Luis underwent surgery to fuse his broken vertebrae. Unfortunately, the surgery had to be halted due to excessive blood loss and the complication of his other lung collapsing. A few days later, four titanium rods were implanted that fused his back from T12 to L4.

For the first week in ICU, Luis's life hung by a thread, and many times experienced doctors and nurses running into the room when his vital signs went flat. To manage the severe pain, he was prescribed a morphine pump at first and then switched to dilaudid, a synthetic version of morphine. But that still wasn't enough, so the medical team added hydrocodone and oxycontin to the pain cocktail. The pain continued to be intense, so his doctors added yet another pain medicine—Neurontin—to the mix to manage the neuropathic pain.

"Nevertheless, they started me with rehab which included physical, occupational, and psychological rehab. In addition, with all the painkillers, all of my bowel system stopped and had to be managed. At that point, all my sense of self evaporated, and in many ways, it felt liberating. And all the lessons I had learned from Byron Katie were allowing me to use every ounce of mental energy for recovery as opposed to "fighting what was."

Rehab was a long journey. Not only did Luis need to learn how to walk again, he also needed to be two months narcotic free before he could reapply for his medical. He was happy to have survived this event, but didn't have insight as to how tough the mental journey was going to be beyond being narcotics free. The hospital became Luis's home, and reality started to set in. What had he done? What had happened began to sink in and the fight back had only just begun.

> At that point, all my sense of self evaporated, and in many ways, it felt liberating.

The Anxious Achiever
Ken, Boeing 767 First Officer

Ken is a thirty-five-year-old white male, a millennial. What started out as a typical afternoon lunch with his dad turned out to be much more than just grabbing a sandwich. He describes it as his day of reckoning, the day when, out of nowhere, he experienced the mother of all anxiety and situational depression attacks.

Ken's story begins when he and his father, Dave, a retired pilot, met for lunch at Subway. Dave ordered his usual, a BLT sub. When the girl asked Ken what he'd like to order, he just stared at her. With a gentle elbow nudge, Dave tried to break Ken's stare and directly posed the question, "Ken, what do you want to eat?" Again, there was no response. Ken later described feeling frozen and numb. He couldn't respond or process words. Then the tears began; lots of tears and uncontrollable crying. What was happening?

Dave guided his son aside and tried to console him. Ken's breathing was labored; his palms, sweaty; his heart, racing. He couldn't stop crying. Ken's father had served in the navy in special ops. The Navy taught breathing techniques for battle that would also serve to keep the soldiers "mind right" in the event they became a POW. Ken's dad began directing Ken in the breathing techniques he learned as a Navy Seal. Eventually, Ken's breathing calmed.

It had taken Ken a tremendous amount of time and passion to become a pilot. His role as pilot was part of his pride and financial security. Retaining "The Right Stuff" was an important part of his image. A nervous breakdown is not what he had in mind. Upon reflection, he admits that the warning signs were there, but it never once crossed his mind that he was on his way to a stress breakdown.

Ken admitted the notion of talking to someone in his airline peer group was a thought that had crossed his mind. "It's similar to asking your best friend what should I do." That sounded reasonable, but cohorts aren't professionals; they are only trained in resources. The fear of exposing his breakdown was not an option. Ken knew he couldn't share what had happened, and the chance that he would self-report was slimmer than hell. If Ken self-reported this event to his aeromedical physician, it just might be the beginning to the end of his career. At the very least, it would be embarrassing, a sign of weakness.

On the other hand, Ken might find himself talking to a flight manager who is by the role that he has obligated to file a report, and a paper trail begins that could be the start of more problems to come. Once the paper trail begins, it is difficult to avoid questions on your next trip to the aeromedical examiner. Ken is one of thousands who don't trust their airline or their union. So, they go underground.

Throwing It All Away
Melinda, Boeing 737 Captain

Melinda still remembers this day as if it was yesterday. Why? It was the day she gave up her wings. She gave herself up to the authorities after a police officer stopped her as she weaved down the street. The police officer witnessed Melinda stumbling and was nearly hit while crossing the street. She had entered a bar the night before, and didn't leave the bar until early morning hours. Her plan was to return to the hotel, sleep it off, and get ready for her scheduled flight that afternoon.

Even the possibility of a flight taking off with an impaired pilot should raise questions for fliers. The responsibility for flagging potentially dangerous behavior falls on many different parties and government agencies, and even pilots themselves. The FAA regulations for commercial pilots are clear—drug and alcohol regulations specifically prohibit pilots from performing flight crewmember duties with prohibited drugs in their systems. They also restrict pilots from flying or attempting to fly an aircraft within eight hours of performing flight crewmember duties, consuming alcohol or if they have an alcohol concentration of 0.04% or greater, pilots may not use alcohol while on-duty or within eight hours of a flight. The regulations also require that crewmembers submit to blood alcohol tests when requested by law enforcement officials authorized to ask for those tests.

So, you might be thinking what brought her to this rock bottom. The stress container that pilots are known for had overflowed. If you were to ask her friends, colleagues and family, if they thought she had an alcohol drinking problem they would have said, "No way." She was considered by her colleagues to be at the top of her game. A good pilot—together, smart. And known as someone who could "hold her liquor." But on the other hand, she couldn't. She wasn't a "now-and-then" drinker who would have a glass of champagne or wine at a celebration or wedding and then not drink again for weeks. Melinda was known as a situational drinker, and she drank between two extremes.

Melinda loved her wine, but what people didn't see was the immediate effects of what red wine delivered. And what people and colleagues didn't see was how easy and frequent that her one glass of wine turned into one bottle a night. As soon as she got to the hotel, she'd find the nearest store that sold alcohol. These are all characteristics of a situational drinker that may be otherwise known as high functional professionals, or functioning alcoholics. There was a time that she stopped drinking alcohol for seven months, another time she stopped for one year, and there were other short periods in between. She felt accomplished, in control, because she was able to stop and start when she wanted to, but the back-and-forth drinking and merry-go-round was the exact thing that she wanted to exit off of that day.

Perhaps you don't relate to this because not everyone will, but I can say for sure that there are people in your life right now, they could be family members, close friends, colleagues, who are rethinking their alcoholic drinking habits. But here's the tricky part. Likely, they are not talking to you about it. And they are not talking to others about it, because they think they can't talk about the elephant in the room, so they go underground. For pilots, they put their livelihood at risk if they openly, honestly talk about it. So, what happens? They suffer. They think that they can handle it alone, until right up the time that they can't. That was Melinda's case. That day her career as a commercial airline pilot came to an end. That day was the first day she became honest with herself and never looked back.

Time in a Bottle
Jim, Boeing 767 First Officer

Jim's teenage years were much like other boys his age. He and his high school buddies would get together on weekend nights and drink beer. They would each grab a six-pack and hang out. After graduating from high school, Jim attended college but wasn't what you would call a strong student. He majored in accounting, but didn't like it much. Jim went to college without any direction, he was not really sure of what he wanted to do or what he wanted in life. Eventually, he talked himself into the idea of doing something worthwhile. By his junior year, he decided that after college his compass pointed to the military. He planned to enlist in the Air Force.

Jim's dad was big on the military. I asked Jim what makes a person go into the military? His answer was "to serve my country." I heard Jim's answer, but what I saw made me think there was more to his answer. What I saw was a man who wanted to make his dad proud.

Jim enlisted for active duty in the marines. He graduated from Officer Candidate School (OCS) and went off to flight school. When flight training was over, his commitment to the military was seven and a half years. The military expects a lot of their soldiers when a person becomes an active-duty pilot. I asked him to tell me more. He shared that the complexity of flight tasks are often associated with high peaks of work and long hours that can create tremendous work overload. I sensed that this was important for me to understand, not only because it was a significant stressor but also—as Jim said—if it persists, there is a clear potential pathway to general stress and fatigue.

He went on to say there were a number of contributing factors to increased workload—night flights, landings and multiple takeoffs, different time zones, all of which can be aggravated by emergencies, in-flight malfunction, or weather difficulties. Honestly, it sounded like the life of any airline pilot. What Jim wasn't saying, but I heard, was that all these stressors contributed to compounding stress, which contributed to increasing his alcohol intake.

After receiving his naval aviator wings in May 1982, Jim confesses that he began to start drinking more and more. Knowing that his father was a fully functioning alcoholic, the likelihood that Jim would follow this cycle was high, yet he still drank.

"Looking back on life is 20/20 vision has deep meaning for me. In the military, there were three incidents that contributed to my demise that I was destined to experience: twice ejected from a jet and my son's death."

Jim's first aviation incident was while flying a Grumman A-6 Intruder, a twin jet attack aircraft. As a junior officer, Jim was the pilot in command, and his bombardier/navigator was a full-bird colonel. They were flying at high speed and low level when they had to eject from the jet.

Jim shared that his whole body suffered trauma from this ejection. His leg was shattered and the flight surgeons were talking about amputation. He recounted how awful this was, but as awful as it was, he survived. But the colonel did not. Jim took a long pause. I could see his eyes soften; he shared, "Maybe if we had ejected earlier, the colonel would be alive. He left behind a wife and kids."

In 1985, Jim again ejected from the Navy TA4J Skyhawk trainer. Back in the day, ejection and surviving was no big deal. Even though it was considered an emergency procedure, doing so didn't include post trauma recovery programs. Sucking it up was considered part of the job. Only the weak needed counseling; so, it was understood—don't whine. You would think that these two incidents would serve to awaken Jim to be more cautious. It didn't. In fact, Jim's wife Peg often proclaimed that Jim was behaving even more carelessly and crazy than ever before. He kept acting out. Part of the survivor's guilt is questioning why one person survived and the other person died. This feeling lives with him every day.

After coming back to the line, he was in a training squadron and was back drinking with the guys. He confessed that deep inside, thoughts of guilt festered concerning the accident that led to the death of the colonel. Both ejection incidents were not Jim's fault. Jim kept saying over and over, "It wasn't my fault, it wasn't my fault." If only he hadn't delayed ejecting, if only he had ejected earlier, the colonel would have made it. Everyone told Jim that the accident was not his fault, but he still carried the trauma.

PTSD is defined as a flashback of events, yet Jim said he doesn't have any flashbacks. PTSD isn't itself harmful. What science tells us is when PTSD is kept bottled up all inside it becomes harmful. Unconsciously or consciously holding emotions inside serves as a placeholder for pain and guilt. An image that came to my mind as he described his emotions was a murky, filthy pond where the sludge at the bottom lived deep painful feelings and emotions.

Those layers of "sludge" are your repressed thoughts, beliefs, and emotions. I've learned the only way to release their power over me is for me to bring each layer up to the surface and feel the pain of what they represent.

Sounds easy; but it isn't. Men have emotions, but they just don't talk about them. Typically, talking with a friend or other pilots is a great start, but most times, especially in Jim's case, it took years of facing his failures in therapy. Trauma affected Jim so much that he left the military and took a few years off from flying. Then the day came when he decided that he did not want to be a pilot any longer.

He took advantage of the program the military offers. A program that promotes a way out if a person wants to "opt out"' for medical reasons. He thought of a new job in sales or operations, but neither one kept his interest. Jim told everyone the reason he left the military was because he did not want to be away from family and friends any longer, yet he kept his foot in the door, by joining a reserve unit where pilots would remind him that being an airline pilot is the best part-time job in the world!

Though four years later, Jim decided to take another stab at becoming an airline pilot. His next goal was to get hired by a major passenger airline. However, there was one big problem. Four years of not flying made Jim's chances of getting hired slim. Clearly, he was noncurrent and hadn't set foot in an airplane in years. That's what Jim needed, though—a new goal—get hired! He stopped drinking alcohol for three months; started a cardio program; and ate healthy food. After passing the "astronaut" physical—he was hired! Setting a goal, again—getting a job done was accomplished.

But something was still wrong. Subconsciously, he continued fighting his emotions. Psychologists call it "suppressing emotions." I call it "filling up his compartment." His PTSD and survivor's guilt compounded and his alcohol drinking increased. But there was one person who was on to him—his wife, Peg. She reminded him constantly that he was drinking alcohol a lot more again. In years past he mostly drank beer, but over the years switched to a more sophisticated drink—spiced rum and diet coke!

As with life, there is a journey and a destination. The secret to life is to enjoy the journey, whatever that will be, because once at the destination—once I "pay off the house," or in Jim's case, "once I get that big airline job"—everything will be wonderful. Yet he continued drinking and flying. Two years after landing his "big-airline job," Jim was furloughed.

Life gives you many zigs and zags; rarely is there a straight line. And a year later, Jim was hired by another major airline as a flight engineer on the Boeing 727. Even though cargo airlines today fly twenty-four seven, thirty years ago, cargo flew primarily at night—all night. We called it the graveyard shift. It's miserable. Any one who has ever worked the graveyard shift knows it's not fun. You never get used to it, you just accept it. This included Jim. He never liked it, but he needed a job. A brand-name cargo airline wanted to hire him, so he was going. He was usually able to control his drinking to the nightly six-pack, but not always. After gaining seniority, he upgraded to the right seat, first officer position, and then, some years later, the left seat of the 727 fleet.

"And it wasn't atypical that, after landing at the intended destination, I found a "place" that would serve breakfast and breakfast beers!" Jim confesses that he typically "only" had two beers for breakfast at one particular "diner" in Harrisburg, Pennsylvania; it became his habit.

It is said that the structure of habits comforts us, and the specialness of ritual revitalizes us. That was Jim. He was somewhere between the habit of alcohol comforting him and revitalizing him.

According to the NHI, it typically takes a person eleven years to reach out for help. So, after some years, Jim finally decided to go underground and "discreetly" make an appointment with a psychologist who diagnosed him with dysthymia, a chronic form of depression.

Since goals inspire Jim, in the spring of 2008, Jim decided he needed another goal—this time it was AIRBUS training. Unlike goal setting for past training cycles, Jim did not stop drinking. In fact, his drinking increased nightly to the point that he was not able to perform his duties as the pilot-in-command student. In civilian talk that means he was the captain, the one who signs for and is responsible for a $150 million jet. He was showing up for training unprepared, hitting an all-time low. He said that it's through the grace of God that he knew that he was at an all-time low. He had no one to talk with outside of a few trusted "buddies" in the airline. He saw no way out except to call in sick and end this training cycle. For the first time, Jim, in his mind, had failed.

"And it wasn't atypical that, after landing at the intended destination, I found a "place" that would serve breakfast and breakfast beers!"

He couldn't do it anymore. His intention was to go home, study some more, and return but that never happened.

"Looking back on the six years between 727 training and the Airbus training, his drinking gradually increased. One time he returned home from a weeklong all-night pairing and waking up at 0300, Jim was ready to go. "I am awake." So, he'd start drinking alcohol! At first, he told himself that he enjoyed the taste of the beer and the little buzz that the beer provided; though, looking back, he understand now, it was part of the depression festering deep inside, the layers of sludge living at the bottom of my emotional pond—the sludge that was making his mind sick."

Somewhere along the way, Jim went from being a "social" drinker to drinking alone. Near the end, he preferred isolation drinking—for two years. In his basement, in his garage, sitting in his truck after working out at the YMCA, alone was anywhere that he could make it. It was after his blood pressure spiked that he figured out: "Hey, this is a great way to go out—hypertension!" No questions asked. So, he did.

Since Jim now had "time on his side," he decided to be honest with his primary care doctor and let him know what was going on and how he had been feeling depressed. Jim also wanted to stop drinking but couldn't. He tried exercise, talk therapy, and supplements (including herbal supplements like St. John's Wort and SAMe), but he was too far along and nothing worked for him. The time had come for him to bare his soul to his family, the FAA, and his company. There was no way out of this now.

Jim was not suicidal, but he was depressed. Jim had hope that antidepressants would be prescribed for a short time, then, he'd get off and back to work for him. He thought he had three doors to open. Door one - could he "live and die by the code of silence and not self report"? Door two - he kept having crazy ideas that he would be able to hide his depression and alcohol by just not self-reporting.

Many times he said, "That's what I'll do!"

Door three - was it more dangerous navigating a transport airplane while secretly self-medicating with the SSRI, or was it more dangerous to navigate an airplane without medication, or self- medicating and being a danger to public health? Jim kept going back and forth, up and down, and every which way trying to justify what "door" he was going to open. Finally, he opened the door with the SSRI behind it and, in 2009, was evaluated and prescribed Lexapro for three months—on the QT. However, Lexapro didn't work well for him and eventually was taken off of this medication.

While Jim was under doctors care to find the medication that would work, much was going on at home. Jim had two sons. His eldest son, Jimmy, succumbed to his death by a drug overdose in his bedroom in his sleep in their home on a Sunday afternoon. Jim reflects back on this day holding back the tears. "I was on my way to church. The new pastor was having a luncheon, and Peg was already at the church helping with the preparation for the event. Before I departed for church, though, I heard Jimmy's alarm going off in his bedroom." As young men typically do sleep in late, initially nothing crossed Jim's mind other than Jimmy had just overslept.

I knew that my son was fighting his own demons, but not this.

Jimmy was working a second shift for a pharmaceutical company. For a guy who didn't go to college, the job was good for him. Everyone liked him, and he had a steady paycheck coming in. When Jim walked into his son's room, Jimmy was in his bed and appeared to be sleeping. However, the first thing that Jim noticed was the blood from Jimmy's nose on his pillow.

"At first, I thought he just had a bloody nose. But as I approached his bed he was stiff—rigor mortis had already begun to set in. I knew that my son was fighting his own demons, but not this. Over the years, Peg and I had thought that he was making progress, baby steps—but not so."

Jim speaks:

"So, what did I do in the next four years before I returned to work? I drank twenty-four seven. I spiraled; My friends and family said I was drinking heavily to numb the pain; I think I was committing a slow suicide. I hid the liquor everywhere. Peg is not one to be fooled. You can't pull the wool over her eyes. Her father drank, but stopped; mine never stopped. I remember one Father's Day about three years after Jimmy died, my second son, Kevin, called me out on my excessive drinking. We both cried. After that I stopped drinking—for a week—but I was miserable in my head. Not only did I have sweats at night, I was withdrawn, without any medical help.

My wife kept telling me I was in denial. I kept telling her, 'I don't drink as much as you think I do.' It was a lie. When I was around her, I was on good behavior, but when she would go to bed, or I was alone, I would drink—a lot. I went on disability and fell off the radar at my airline. I started to go to a mental health provider but paid out of pocket.

My wife, Peg, was finally relieved that I was seeking the help that I had resisted for years. Peg knew for years I was drinking too much. I was not violent with Peg, but I was subtly demeaning toward her. I want to talk about my verbal abuse towards her. It was wrong, and to this day it deeply shames me. It brings me pain. I talked to her disrespectfully, I ignored her, I was unloving, and made up stories. For years, she told me to get help. I told her that I would, and I did occasionally, sometimes as long as a few years, but nothing really changed my habits and behaviors.

I trusted my mental health professionals, yet I still was in complete denial, which aided my story. Truly I did not want to stop. No, I did want to stop, but couldn't. Now I know that I was sick in my mind. To this day, I continue to make amends to Peg. She is the reason that I am here today. A counselor once asked me to remember one sobering thought a day. And I have plenty of them when it comes to Peg.

I want to give back and be someone that my family and friends are proud of. Some people have fair weather friends, I have all weather friends. They know I will be there for them also. Part of the recovery is that you do it for yourself. I did it for me, but I stay sober for my family and friends. I do not want to let them down again.

The pivoting point for me started when I hit bottom. Peg, through a friend of hers, shared that her husband, a Delta pilot, had a good result after he made a call to his airline to enter the HIMS (Human Intervention Management System) program. I thought, what do I have to lose, because I was heading toward throwing everything away. The truth is my alcoholism was beyond my control. I needed intervention. It wasn't until after four years of drinking daily, I called a recovered alcoholic, and decided to enter the HIMS program. Reaching for the phone, dialing the number and connecting to someone that could help, someone that I could trust, started my journey with HIMS, which keeps me honest and true to me, my family, and my friends.

I had to get honest with my failures and fears. The HIMS program was established to provide a system whereby afflicted pilots are treated and successfully returned to the cockpit under the FAA Special Issuance Regulations. I found I could be totally honest with fellow pilots in the HIMS program. Some are even recovering addicts. It's important to confess that at times I couldn't always be totally honest with the HIMS administrators. It took me seven and a half years to return to flying, not as a captain, but as a first officer. The stress is so much less. It was at HIMS where I received my double diagnosis of depression and alcoholism.

I'm one of the lucky ones. Today I'm prescribed one of the four SSRIs (antidepressants) approved by the FAA to help me battle with my depression. Some are not as lucky. I still attend AA meetings. The FAA position on SSRIs is to some extent they would rather have a pilot on medication, monitored rather than a pilot flying without medication, or worse self-medicating, but that is only to some extent. SSRI are deemed safe for pilots and the general population. One of my FAA requirements under the FAA Special Issuance Regulations is to connect with my fleet captain. Due to COVID-19, now I must phone in. The HIMS program follows recovering alcoholics; peer monitoring that I report to monthly which is similar to a sponsor for AA.

I've finally brought the emotions and feelings that live at the bottom of my murky filthy pond up to the top and faced them—straight on. It hurt, it was painful. But it had to be done. The lurking sludge doesn't go away, it's just accepted. Anything can trigger them, but they can't hurt me any longer, unless, that is, I allow them too."

These stories are but a few snapshots into the lives of countless airline pilots who have found themselves in situations where they are fighting terrible mental-health battles, and they feel alone. It doesn't have to be this way. My heart breaks thinking of the lost years and lost potential suffered by people, including pilots and air traffic controllers who felt trapped and could see no way out. Resorting to self-destructive coping mechanisms destroys families, lives, and careers.

When we hide, we force ourselves into trying to navigate impossible situations without instruments to guide us. Some of the above stories had positive outcomes, some not so positive. They can serve as wake up calls, opening our hearts to the inherent struggles of humanity that we all share.

SIX
AT WHAT COST

Seventy-five percent of all mental illness cases can be found in low-income countries. However, stress, anxiety, alcohol, depression (SAAD) can be also found in high-income nations and high performance professions such as pilots and air traffic controllers, lawyers, doctors, and for that matter anyone whose "compartment" has overflown. What is tricky is that the container measure is different for each and everyone of us.

Even before COVID-19, anxiety and depression were estimated to cost the global economy over $1 trillion every year in lost productivity. With the global wellness market forecast to reach $66 BILLION by 2022, it is clear that organizations may be spending money on reactive programs rather than preventative education (i.e., mental health awareness training).

Globally, we invest less than 1% of preventative resources and time on mental health and self-care.

A report from UC Davis indicates stresses that develop into depression and anxiety have increased 35% in the last four years. According to current research from the World Health Organization

(WHO), the forecast for global spending on mental health care is $7.8 trillion. Research from the Global Wellness Institute suggests that mental health is now a $45 trillion industry, up from $3.7–$4.2 trillion between the years 2015 to 2017.

> Globally, we invest less than 1% of preventative resources and time on mental health and self-care.

According to the Anxiety and Depression Association of American, National Institute of Mental Health, World Economic Forum, and National Alliance on Mental Illness:

- Depressions rank among the most common causes of disability in the United States. Eighteen percent of United States adults—some forty million people—have anxiety disorders, the most prevalent mental illness.
- Forty-three percent of United States adults with mental illness have received mental health services within the past year.
- Sixty-seven percent of United States adults with a personality disorder have at least one other mental illness.
- It is two to four times as likely that offspring of a depressed parent will develop depression.
- One in twenty-five United States adults has a serious mental illness that limits or interferes with major life activities.
- Six trillion dollars is the projected annual global cost of mental disorder projected for 2030—more than the combined cost of diabetes and cancer.
- Sixteen million United States adults have experienced at least one major depressive episode in the past year.

The world economic forum in the Harvard School of Public Health estimates from 2011 to 2030, major diseases and mental illness are estimated at today's cost at $47 trillion to the global economy, and we're only in 2020.

In the published paper, *Mental Health Stigma Update: A Review of Consequence*, evidence was found that suggested that 46.6% of all adults in American will experience a mental disorder in their lifetime. A person would be quite foolish to think that commercial pilots are on the better side of those statistics.[9]

Don't get me wrong. I'm not implying that stress and burnout cause all disease and mental illness, but think about it: if only a portion of this cost is relevant, imagine how much lower that number could be.

Here's something else to think about: Canada's population is almost exactly the population of the state of California. It is shocking to learn that the impact of mental health problems and illness is more than one-and-a-half times that of all cancers in Canada.

In 2012, 38% of people in Canada had a family member with a mental health problem or illness. Five hundred thousand Canadians, including those who work in healthcare, will not make it to work in any given week because of a mental health problem or mental illness. This has an impact on the workplace through heightened absenteeism, reduced productivity, and increased cost—much of which could be avoided by ensuring a mentally healthy workplace.

The cost of mental health problems and illnesses to the Canadian economy has been estimated to be well in excess of $50 billion—a figure equivalent to 2.8% of Canada's Gross Domestic Product—of which $20 billion stems from the workplace. One in three disability claims in Canada is related to mental illness and the numbers are growing. Mental health claims represent 70% of the total cost of disability claims. This is partly because a person dealing with a mental health issue is likely to be off work much longer than someone dealing with another type of disability. That's the tricky part about mental illness versus physical illness. If a person breaks his or her arm, they know it. It hurts. There's the cast. You can see it. With mental illness, the signs and symptoms are not seen, they are internal. And unless the person who is suffering has a heightened state of awareness or sensations to the body, warning signs are often ignored.

Mental illness costs the private sector between $180–$300 billion in short-term disability and $135 billion for long-term disability. Absenteeism and presenteeism due to mental health issues account for more than $6 billion in lost productivity.

SEVEN
A BELIEVABLE ACT

About 40 million adults deal with an anxiety disorder at any given time, according to the National Institute of Mental Health. Of this, approximately 18% of the population falls into the category of "high functioning," which is, essentially, silent anxiety hidden behind a smile.

A pilot suffering from functioning anxiety may be the picture of success. He or she might arrive at work earlier than everyone else, impeccably uniformed, hair neatly styled. Fellow colleagues may know them as driven in their work; never missing a day of work or falling short in a given task. Not only that, they are always willing to help others when asked. Their social schedule also seems busy and full, yet they might crave alone time.

If you have high-functioning anxiety, you probably notice that your anxiety propels you forward rather than leaving you frozen in fear, sweats, or gasping for air. On the surface, you likely appear to be successful, together, and calm—the classic type A personality who excels at work and in life—although the way you actually feel on the inside may be very different. You may appear calm on the outside, yet a "hamster" wheel is turning inside.

As I have mentioned, pilots are known as great compartmentalizers, a trait that can become physically harmful. Pilots are not always good judges of their abilities. For example, many sleep-deprivation and workload studies claim that stress and fatigue can produce effects similar to those of a person under the influence of alcohol. Both of these common mental and physical states, when taken beyond the limits of the pilot, deprive him or her of proper phasic and tonic alertness.

When stressors are packed too tightly into a given compartment, it eventually overflows and it's no surprise when life gets messy.[10]

Stress can manifest itself through symptoms of physical diseases such as respiratory, digestive, hormonal, as well as SAAD. We can no longer afford to think of workplace health and safety from only a physical perspective.

Since doctors have had the authority to temporarily or permanently ground a pilot, pilots have always been leery of doctors, and even more so of psychologists. In fact, pilots don't have to search too far for the latest gouge on how to pass a flight physically. Tools that pilots use are forums or websites explaining how to pass an aviation medical exam.[11] Additionally, there are online pilot forums threads providing advice on medical issues[12] and pilot unions taking positions and offering support to pilot with concerns of medical issues.[13] The bottom line is that it's the pilot's responsibility to self-report stress maladies with the understanding it may negatively impact their job.

Every six months when commercial airline transport pilots report for their Class I aviation medical, they know that successfully passing this exam is a prerequisite to keeping their jobs. They have invested tens of thousands of dollars and have completed thousands of training and required flight hours to get to this point in their careers. For a pilot suffering from mental health issues, if the pilots divulge negative information about their emotional or mental states, their livelihoods are instantly put in jeopardy. Continuing to work depends upon their ability to put on a *believable act*. For the duration of the office visit, a silent mantra repeats—just sign the damned paper.

Let's take a peek into the exam room after the doctor walks in:

Doctor: Hi Joe, how's it going?

Pilot: Oh it's good, man! Better than the alternative!

Doctor: So, how are you? Are you having any concerns? How's the home life? Finances? Are the kids ok?

Pilot: No issues, man—I'm good!

Doctor: How's your stress? Sleeping well? Are you exercising?

Pilot: Stress? I go to work to get unstressed! (LAUGH)

The entire time Joe is thinking, "Doc, even if I were having any negative thoughts or struggles, I sure as *hell* wouldn't tell you! Just sign the damned paper and get me out of here!"

The origins of the fraught relationship between pilots and doctors goes back to the beginning of aviation. One hundred years ago, physiological facets were used for military purposes. There was a damn good reason for such suspicion concerning the first test that decided the future of candidate pilots. Professional and mental examinations were based upon the candidate's written answers to a series of questions covering his parentage, education, business experience, athletic attainments, responsibilities, and military training. In today's aviation world, this would be unheard of, not to mention illegal. However, due to the demands of the war, this method was the best they had in place and was accepted.

In spite of good intentions, and due to the demands of war, there were more protocols in regards to pilot mental health that supported a pilot perspective of suspicion towards doctors and psychologists. During the RAF bombing campaign in WWII the term "lack of moral fiber" was used to blame, shame and punish "weaklings and waivers" (Harris, 1940, p. 1) into continuing to fly in the face of high losses of aircraft and crew as well as increasing psychiatric casualties.[4]

The pride that has always been a part of the aviation profession was used against the psychology of pilots. Still, today the threat of losing professional and social stance has a great impact on a pilot's psyche. The ego blow of potentially losing status, combined with an ingrained suspicion of doctors, continues to create difficulties between pilots and health care professionals to this day.[4]

So, here we are at the crossroads again. How can pilots or air traffic controllers receive the mental health care treatment that is afforded to other high performance professionals without the barriers or fears of losing their professional license? The bottom line—they can't, due to the current legislation. Until industry and the public push for reforming outdated mental health regulations, the only thing we have is choice, education, resources and redemption. In the following chapters, I'd like to offer some strategies that can help you chart a course toward that redemption. Some may think of redemption only in a religious context, but redemption can be used in the action of buying one's freedom. In this case, it means having the freedom to educate yourself of the many options available that can help empower you to create well-being and good health in your life. The choice has always been yours.

PART II
PILOT IN COMMAND

EIGHT
MY STORY

It was a beautiful autumn day when I walked into my doctor's office expecting a routine wellness check. The intake nurse entered the exam room, asked a few friendly questions, reached for my left arm and wrapped the blood pressure cuff around my arm. It was one of those digital ones, that in my opinion aren't really accurate, so it didn't surprise me when she said, "Let's try the right arm." I could tell she wasn't happy with the reading and asked if I had taken any type of cold medicine. I shook my head no. I thought, "Does it look like I have a cold, lady?" After the right arm reading, she departed the room and quickly returned with the doctor. I remember the doctor making small talk, I assumed to put me at ease. However, this time it was the doctor who reached for my arm and used the old-fashioned cuff with the sphygmomanometer gauge, the one with the balloon on the end. Next, she looked into my eyes with a small skinny flashlight, while asking me how I felt. I replied fine.

It was then that my world crashed down around me. The doctor announced that I was having a stroke. My blood pressure had skyrocketed to 190/160. I was in a dangerous stroke range and the dilation of my eyes confirmed her statement. I sat on the examining table for what felt like an eternity. I felt my head pounding and my heart racing, I was speechless. Stunned. The doctor asked if I had any questions. I sat there dazed. And the good little servant pilot that I am, the next thing that I did was stand up, like I was on autopilot, and announced, "I'm a very busy woman; I have kids to pick up from school in an hour, and I'm scheduled to go to work tomorrow. I don't have time for this crap!" The look on her face was one of disbelief. She asked if anyone was with me. I said, "NO! Didn't you hear me? I don't have time for this!" She asked if my husband could come and pick me up, I said, "Hell no."

The doctor commanded that I lay down; the office was calling a transport to take me to the ER. She turned off the light, closing the door behind her. What did I do? Within a matter of a minute, I opened the door—looked left and right—and scrammed right out of the office!

I still remember the exact spot where I had parked in my car. I sat in the parking lot and cried, and cried. My head pounded and my heart raced as I faced one of the greatest terrors of my life—losing my medical certificate, which translated into losing the ability to provide for my three children. Finally, I mustered the will to turn the key in my car, shift into reverse, then drive.

Somehow through the grace of God I was able to drive home. I don't remember how I got there, but I do remember how I felt.

That night I laid in my bed, scared as hell. What resources did I have—none. Who can I trust—nobody. Stroke. Hypertension! Where did this come from?

It wasn't until two days later that I came to terms that I needed to see a doctor. I reached out to the only heart doctor that I knew, Dr. Freelan, a well-known cardiologist in my hometown of Pittsburgh. In fact, Dr. Freelan had been my father and mother's cardiologist for years.

Both Tom and Delfina never missed their routinely yearly checkup and throughout the years became somewhat of an unofficial family friend of the doc. The bonus: Doc Freelan was the cardiologist of choice for aviators in Pittsburgh. In the 1980s, US Airways headquarters and their largest crew base was located in Pittsburgh. Aging pilots sought out Dr. Freelan for care. It usually took months to land an appointment, but luckily for me, the front office scheduled an appointment the next day.

After a thorough exam, Dr. F. sat down at his desk as I sat in a chair beside his desk. He didn't beat around the bush with the plan to get me healthy again—drugs! He first explained that high blood pressure is common amongst pilots. He shared that many pilots take high blood pressure medicine and continue to work, but some don't. However, he expected me to be one of the lucky ones. With that, he stroked a prescription on his prescription pad for a blood pressure medicine and slid it across the desk to me. It was his next recommendation that blew me away. He looked at me for what seemed like a few minutes and then said, "You need an anti-anxiety prescription, too." It's called Xanax! With a wink, Doc explained that taking anti-anxiety or antidepressants isn't all that uncommon amongst pilots and there's a community of pilots who could guide me through. I asked, "What do you mean, guide me through?" He looked at me with bewilderment as if to say, "Really, you really don't know?" Then it hit me—how to obtain these without a paper trail. I responded, "I can't do that!"

Reflecting back, my feeling of bewilderment and disbelief was strong, yet I felt anger toward the doctor. I thought, "*Is this the best he can do for me?*" On the other hand, my hypertension was a serious issue and I needed to take steps concerning it for my own health safety. I couldn't understand though why the doc was medically recommending drugs. Was it because of the "don't ask, don't tell" secret handshake in the industry? Or was it more so that it was the easiest step to take? I departed the office with both prescriptions in hand, never to be filled.

I left his office with a container of mixed emotions. How could this be? How could pilots put their job in jeopardy by going down the forbidden road of anti-anxiety prescriptions? Every aviator is well aware of the FAA's stance on mind altering drugs including antidepressants. In fact, prior to 2010 usage of ANY antidepressant usage disqualified a pilot from flying. In April 2010, the FAA publicly came out and approved the use of four SSRIs (Selective Serotonin Reuptake Inhibitor). The catch—the approval is on a case-by-case basis.[4]

SSRI is an antidepressant that works by increasing levels of "feel good" neurotransmitter serotonin within the brain.[4]

But a case-by-case basis is not a guarantee your case would be approved. Then again it hit me. Pilots must be going underground in fear of losing their livelihood.

It just so happened that a week later was my yearly dental hygiene appointment. Before the cleaning began, the dental hygienist and I exchanged small talk. Typically I'm a private person, but today I just blurted out the recent news of my hypertension and anxiety diagnosis. What was an unintentional blurt ended up being one of the luckiest days in my life. The dental hygienist shared that her sister recently was diagnosed with hypertension and discovered a functional medicine doctor who is treating her successfully without drugs. What?! @#$%—I knew that I needed to find her! It was then that I began my first step in the search for new good health pathways and never looked back.

As opposed to the traditional medical system of treating symptoms, functional medicine doctors venture into the frontier of finding the root cause of illness and disease. They discover what the body is lacking, what it needs, and treat disorders from the inside out. This is an alternative type of medicine, but one that has amazing results.

I began seeing Dr. Frannie B. for my hypertension. The initial appointment lasted two and a half hours. After listening to my life story, she ordered unconventional blood, hormone, stool, and saliva tests with an appointment in hand to return for a follow up appointment in 3 weeks. It was through these blood tests that I discovered that the cause of my high blood pressure was high toxicity throughout my body. Mercury to be exact. But what did that mean and where do I go from here?

One thing was for sure: my sleep had to improve. Even though my role as a pilot gave options of night and day flying, I chose night flying because it allowed me to be at home with my children during the day. I understand the stress and pressure it takes to achieve work-life balance, and to take care of our families. But when it comes down to chronic stress and fatigue, do you know what can happen? You can develop irreversible high blood pressure, and eventually lose function of your kidney and spend the rest of your life on dialysis. You could develop heart disease and suppressed digestion, to name a few. I discovered that sleep deprivation and external stressors had a huge impact on my blood pressure and anxiety, too. From that moment on, sleep became a resource that I protected at all cost. I know that if I don't get my sleep, it will impact every organ, in every part of my body.

There is simply no feature of your wellbeing and good health that gets away from sleep deprivation.[4]

Now, about my anxiety: She asked if I ever heard of mindfulness meditation. I said, "Pardon me?" She explained that mindfulness meditation originated in Buddhist traditions, but it's not a religion. It's a breathing practice that relaxes your mind and heals your body. Dr. John Kabat-Zinn, PhD, is a professor of medicine emeritus at the University of Massachusetts Medical School, where he was founding executive director of the Center for Mindfulness in Medicine, Health Care, and Society, and founder (1979) and former director of its world-renown Stress Reduction clinic. He has secularized the practice, and it's making an impact in the West. She explained that meditation focuses on the breath in a deliberate way which reduces stress by increasing the size of the gray matter and reduces the amygdala (fight, fright, freeze) in the brain. It's a practice of healing by relaxing - relaxing your mind heals your body. Given that the year was 2006, long before meditation had gone mainstream, I wasn't sure what to believe at this point. It sounded pretty hocus-pocus to me, yet I was curious.

My curiosity got the better of me (as it usually does). A week later, I drove to Barnes and Nobles and meandered through the self-care section of the store, hoping no one that I knew would see me. Through the many books in the self-care section, a book by Jack Kornfield—*Mindfulness for Beginners*—caught my eye. Still a skeptic, I purchased the book with the intention of proving Dr. Frannie wrong. My mindset was to practice every day and "breathing" (sounded silly!) with discipline with the goal of returning to my three-month appointment, having gathered all the ammunition as to why mindfulness meditation practice *didn't* have an affect on my anxiety.

Much to my surprise, I discovered the exact opposite! I experienced that mindfulness meditation created a way of paying attention, and in turn it made "space" and that awareness rose through paying attention. After three months of meditation practice for ten minutes, three times per day, I was responding to my children differently, I was less reactive, I was more compassionate, and I had more empathy. I was present. Mindfulness meditation stands on its own as a powerful vehicle for self-understanding and healing. Frannie was right—meditation relaxes your mind, and heals your body. Additionally, I discovered another benefit of mindful meditation. You can find your why; make a new start; drop old, deceptive habits; and learn new ones that serve you. This all started for me when I discovered mindfulness.

Meditation it's free. It's mobile. It saved me from succumbing to the conventional mind altering medicines that are prescribed so freely in our culture. All it took from me was breathing in a deliberate way daily.

My dedication to my family and my career was pure perseverance, driven by responsibility and my love for my family, but in reality, I wasn't listening to my body well. And it frequently meant that I ignored signs of chronic stress and exhaustion, and as it turns out it caused me to really be vulnerable to disease physically and emotionally, rather than seeing my body as a trusted and valued partner who is integral to the success of my ability in aviation and ultimately deserving of care.

For decades, I pushed myself beyond my physical and mental limitations. I viewed my body as a disobedient servant. It took me a while to break those habits and the mental thinking of how I approach my body in order to value it for the glorious work that it does and enabling my physical presence in the world. To shift my mindset from instructing a disobedient servant, to listening to an integrated and valued partner, worthy of time, care and compassion, it's been a process and I share this because by changing your mindset, your habits don't necessarily change overnight. It's simple, but not easy.

My thinking patterns about my body were deeply ingrained over years through my beliefs and personal experience. The first step in my journey to recovery was bringing awareness—notice—to habits and my mindset, to the inner monologue, and intentionally choosing a different path forward. While my old mindset can still pop up from time to time and I might experience a feeling of guilt creeping in if I choose to rest or take care rather than continuing on my work, I know now what I need to do to be whole and to live a healthier embodied life for the long haul.

In the following chapters, I share what I've discovered from years of research and adopted lifestyle factors that I found to be fundamental principles in creating wellbeing and good health: sleep and relaxation; exercise and movement; nutrition; managing stress; and relationships that have immeasurably increased the quality of my life. The information and methods presented are easily accessible to anyone with curiosity and a willingness to try something new. I invite you to approach them with a mind open to the possibilities of a healthier, happier future.

NINE
THE POWER OF HABITS

John wakes up each morning to a deluge of stressful thoughts about the day ahead. The moment he opens his eyes, he reaches for his iPhone to scan the long list of push notifications, his inbox, or the latest news that came through overnight. He checks the "open time" for his seat position on the airplane (there must be some juicy trips in there!). Meanwhile his random thoughts may go something like, "Oh yeah, I've got to remember to schedule my first class medical. Did I make the car appointment for a tune up? And I have to pay the yearly taxes which are overdue!" "Today I need to pick up the kids at 3:00!" Already overwhelmed, he spends the next thirty minutes distracting himself by watching or listening to the morning news. At the last minute, before rushing out the door, he reads the latest blog posts on a range of light topics, from entertainment to who is where these days. Not surprisingly, the rest of John's day matches his morning. The stress of the day has already started compounding. His day is rushed, he feels hurried, his mind wanders all over the place, and he's relieved when it finally comes to an end.

On the other hand, Grant wakes up with a similar torrent of

stressful thoughts. But instead of opening his email or checking text messages on his iPhone, he questions stressful thoughts, and spends the next ten minutes practicing mindfulness meditation. Centering. Some days, he'll sit in silence for ten minutes, or he'll stretch before getting ready for work without any thoughts. No morning news. No noise. If he does have racing thoughts (some call it "monkey mind"), he notices them and says "Ahhh, there it is again—the mind has a mind of its own. It's doing what it does, Grant notices and gently brings his mind back to centering - his breath. By the time Grant is ready to walk out his door, his body feels refreshed and energized, his mind is open and awake. Similar to John, the rest of Grant's day matches his morning. In Grant's case, it's calm, productive, stimulating, yet engaging. His well-being is balanced.

The takeaway of the two stories is that good practices lead to good habits. Good habits form the foundation of well-being. This isn't anything new. A couple thousand years ago, Aristotle said, "Moral excellence comes about as a result of habit." The nineteenth-century American psychologist William James also understood that we need habits. Without them, we couldn't shower, get dressed, brush our teeth, or find our way to the grocery store. "Habit," he observed, "simplifies our movements, makes them accurate, and diminishes fatigue."[14]

Habits work to increase efficiency in the brain and body. They allow us to go on autopilot while completing so-called mindless tasks such as washing dishes, walking down a flight of stairs, opening the mail, or tying our shoes.[14] Think of life without habits—a life spent relearning these mundane tasks over and over. Life would be slow, frustrating, and vastly inefficient. So far, so good—right? Well, not so fast. Habits come at a price. By making our actions instinctive, even mindless, habits sometimes take away our conscious power to choose and can limit our options.

Let's talk about the other end of the spectrum regarding habits—bad habits. Come on, you have them! I have them, we all have them.

The majority of us have some habitual vice. It might be eating junk food, smoking, Starbucks runs every morning, drinking a few beers or glasses of wine to wind down every night, or looking at our iPhone or iPad first thing in the morning. We all know what it feels like to be drawn to something out of habit. We know how easy it is to eat an entire pint of Ben & Jerry's ice cream without choosing to do so. In these situations, the "efficiency" of habit overcomes our capacity to choose. The brain switches to autopilot, with our bad habit at the controls.

In subtle, seemingly innocuous ways, this happens all . . . dayyyy . . . long. For example, on your day off, you'll get up, have coffee, work out, shower, eat breakfast, then you're ready for your day. The cockpit setup is done in one way only—pilots call it SOP. I'm not saying this is bad, what I am saying is that, even though it's efficient, its ingrained chain of habits can also make change difficult.

Let's circle back to William James's big idea about habits. While our habits often control us, we can learn how to control them by exerting conscious choice. Like today's neuroscientists, James viewed our habits as plastic, or malleable. In his words, "Plasticity, then, in the widest sense of the word, means weak enough to yield to an influence, but strong enough not to yield all at once." In other words, we can't change all of our habits overnight, but through conscious practice, we can slowly rewire the system with new, more productive habits.[14]

When I was in coursework and studying at Brown University, the teachers would use the analogy of superhighways in our brains. Without conscious awareness, our actions will quickly follow the high-speed route of habit. But through practice, we can exit the freeway and drive onto new roads, new neural pathways, that are less efficient. However, the more we drive on these new pathways, the wider and more traversable they become. It becomes easier to turn off the habitual superhighway of destructive habits.[14]

The key is conscious awareness? Just *noticing*. Noticing is where change starts. When we become aware of our habits, we can then choose whether to follow our usual, unconscious conditioning or chart a new pathway of habit. James insisted, "My experience is what I agree to attend to. Only those items which I notice shape my mind."[14]

The idea that we can use our attention to train the habits of well-being is no longer just a philosophical premise. When James wrote *Habit* in 1890, he was ahead of this time. Today, one of the hottest areas of neuroscience research is neuroplasticity. By using fMRI scans and other imaging techniques, we now have clear empirical evidence to support James's theory. It is indeed possible to train the brain the same way we train our bodies.[14]

Neuroplasticity is a game changer. For hundreds of years, scientists have assured us that, once we reach adulthood, the structures of the brain and nervous system are fixed.[14] We've all heard the old saying, "You can't teach an old dog new tricks." They thought the brain was like plaster—pliable at first, but hardening over time. Psychiatrist Norman Doidge explained, "The common wisdom was that after childhood the brain changed only when it began the long process of decline." Since the brain could not change, human nature, which emerges from it, seemed necessarily fixed and unalterable as well.[14]

Today, driven by scientific discovery, a new and more optimistic picture has emerged. The brain is less like plaster and more like plastic. It can be changed and transformed in previously unimaginable ways. Dr. Richard Davidson, founder and director of the Center for Healthy Minds at the University of Wisconsin, explained, "The brain has the ability to change its structure and patterns of activity in significant ways not only in childhood but also in adulthood and throughout life."[14]

Have you ever heard of the term *neurons that fire together, wire together*? This exciting discovery dates back to the pioneering work of psychologist Donald Hebb in the late 1940s. By shifting our habitual thought patterns and behaviors, we activate and establish new neural structures in the brain and rewire the brain to create a new set of habits.[14]

Neuroanatomist Jill Bolte Taylor expressed the difference between habitual thought and intentional thought this way, "Your body is the life force power of some fifty trillion molecular geniuses. You alone choose, moment by moment, who and how you want to be in the world. I encourage you to pay attention to what is going on in your brain. Own your power and show up in your life."[14]

Taylor touches on one of the primary themes running throughout well-being: the idea that from one moment to moment to the next, we choose how to direct our attention. We can choose to let the ordinary habits of the mind fly the airplane, allowing stress and tension to take us to our usual destination. Or we can choose to redirect our attention—to train our minds, focus to experience a more optimal state of well-being.

The idea of awareness or noticing lies at the center of well-being. In each of the subjects discussed in the following chapters—sleep and relaxation, nutrition, managing stress, movement and exercise, relationships, and the power of a good night's sleep, you will learn foundational, practical, and transformable new pathways by making conscious choices. You'll learn to redirect your attention and begin to "shape" your mind and develop habits that will "re-shape" your life through lifestyle changes. Just like it did for me and countless others.

TEN
RELAX YOUR MIND, HEAL YOUR BODY

The science is clear. Mindfulness meditation changes the very structure of the brain, reducing stress and promoting overall well-being and good health. Because of the overwhelming body of evidence to support the benefits of mindfulness meditation, this is where well-being begins.

> *"I've been meditating for two years now and it's the best thing I have ever done to help bring more creativity, positive energy, and peace to my life. When I'm tired, stressed, anxious, or depressed, I meditate, and it clears my mind and makes me feel relaxed and happier. I have shared the meditation experience with my friends and recommended it to everyone that I know."*[14]

These aren't the words of a Buddhist monk or a guru. These are the words of the American pop icon Katy Perry. But Katy Perry is not alone: Jeff Weiner, CEO of LinkedIn; Wm Clay Ford, Chairman and CEO; Marc Benioff, chairman and CEO of Salesforce; Arianna Huffington, co-founder of Huffington Post; Oprah Winfrey, media proprietor, actress, and philanthropist; Congressman Tim Ryan, Russell Simmons, and Paul McCarthy join the list.[14]

When Oprah introduced meditation into her company the results were, in her words, "Awesome: Better sleep. Improved relationships with spouses, children, coworkers. Some people who once suffered with pain don't anymore. Greater productivity and creativity all around."[14]

Meditation is considered mainstream now, but it wasn't always this way. Fifty years ago, this ancient practice was positioned at the fringe of popular culture. To most people in the western world, meditation seemed weird, exotic, and foreign. However, thankfully today meditation now occupies a very different place in science and popular culture. At technology companies like Google, mindfulness meditation has become a central practice for boosting productivity, reducing workplace drama, and sparking creativity. Even NFL teams, like the Seattle Seahawks, have begun using meditation as a tool to enhance performance on the field.

Within the scientific community, the meditation research of Dr. Richard Davidson and others is no longer viewed with disdain. Instead, this research has added significantly to the *rapidly* growing scientific literature on neuroplasticity, the amazing ability of the human brain to keep learning, growing, and changing.

Since the roots of today's mindfulness practices began in the East, some people mistakenly view mindfulness as a religion. It is not. The systemic cultivation of meditation has been the heart of Buddhism. It has flourished for more than 2,600 years in monastic and secular settings in many Asian countries.

In the 1960s and 1970s, the practice of this kind of meditation became much more widespread worldwide and the trend has even gotten stronger in the past thirty years. In fact, there has been an explosion just in the past few years. Today, Mindfulness Based Stress Reduction (MBSR) is finding its way into global mainstream society at an accelerating rate. And as I previously stated, Ford, Google, Sales Force, Intel and J.P.Morgan are just a handful of corporations that have brought mindfulness meditation into their corporate culture.

One of the major strengths of specialized mindfulness programs such as Mindfulness Based Stress Reduction (MBSR) and Mindfulness Based Cognitive Therapy (MBCT) are that they are not dependent on any belief system or ideology. Their potential benefits of the practices are accessible for anyone to test for him or herself.

Having deep roots in Catholicism, I can understand skepticism. When my functional medicine doctor first introduced me to the concept of meditation, I thought it was religion; and I was determined to prove her wrong in regards to its scientific benefits. But MBSR is simply a practice that can adapt to new contexts.

For example, in Europe (EU) many if not all cultures practice eating meals that can last hours. That is not the case in America where dining is typically rushed—in and out. Does that mean that Americans can't enjoy a dining experience for hours? Of course not. From my point of view, mindfulness is adaptable to any situation which happens to be the one in which the participants find themselves. My fascination is to explore how mindfulness applies to aviation performance, and enhances well-being and overall good health.

SCIENTIFIC EVIDENCE

Mindfulness practice is evidence-based, and scientific links have been made between meditation and emotional fitness. It has been proven to reduce the reactive part of the brain and expand the reasoning part. Meditation doesn't just change the brain; it also changes the body by enhancing the immune systems. In recent years, a growing body of research from Dr. Richard Davidson shows that mediation delivers additional compelling benefits key to our performance in most life activities and overall functioning including:[14]

- Increased focus. Meditation activates additional circuits in the brain that allows for sharper and more efficient concentration.[14]
- Enhanced pain tolerance. After five months of meditation practice, subject response to pain in the thalamus decreased by 40–50%.[14]
- Decreased mind wandering. Meditation reduces moments when our attention wanders away from what is happening in the present.[14]
- Slower mental aging. As we age, the density of gray matter decreases. But meditation appears to counteract this effect by increasing the density of gray matter in the brain, rendering the brain more facile in old age.[14]

Mindfulness meditation, coupled with a willingness to be honest, courageous, and put a plan into action may be just the **start** you need. A consistent practice not only develops beneficial qualities such as reducing stress, *increasing focus*, slowing mental aging, and increasing pain tolerance, it also expands your capacity to love, have compassion, and feel empathy.[14]

Mindfulness helps a person maintain stability while moving through the challenges of life. Stress related to the aviation profession, buying a house, welcoming a new child, and getting married or divorced are common stressors. These common stressors are only the tip of the iceberg, but what about below the iceberg? What about the uncommon stressors that many suffer from and yet go undiagnosed? A stable platform cultivated through mindfulness practice can help an individual navigate life's inevitable stresses and reduce the chances of spiraling into chronic stress, anxiety, or depression.

This doesn't happen overnight. For me, it took one year of small, yet consistent, new habits to build my new neural pathways. Pathways that I find today were so well worth the time invested. Sometimes there can be the expectation that mindfulness practices will bring peace, bliss, joy, and the sense that "everything is going to be great in the world again." There is so much to acknowledge as to what is in the practice of mindfulness. You become aware of difficult or negative emotions and do not push them away. You don't try to contrive a "positive" mood in high stress circumstances. You just allow the emotions to be here. When a strong experience happens, you embrace it. For me, it was when my mother passed away from pancreatic cancer: I did not see it as any other way than just sad. Just sad. And I leaned into emotion. I'm having this emotion, a feeling; and, like everything else, with time, this feeling will pass.

In some sense, this part of the practice is a form of distress tolerance. If we train the mind with open monitoring and allow emotions to appear like a cloud—letting it pass away and trying not to hold on to anything, we stay more steady as those difficult emotions come and go. That steadiness is more powerful and more beneficial than feeling happy for a few moments.

ATTENTION TRAINING FOR HIGH PERFORMANCE

Mindfulness can help those in high-performance, high-demanding professions (firefighters, ICU nurses, military, commercial pilots, etc.). What we know is that everything gets worse at the end rather than at the beginning. I've seen this time and time again as I align this with my own experience as a pilot. When stress levels and negative moods are higher, you feel the least clear and well. You feel the worst at the exact moment you need to perform. There is denigration in performance over the course of a demanding situation, right at the critical moments when performance can least afford to suffer. I'm thinking about every take off and landing.

I often hear, "Is this mindfulness just attention or focus training?" I responded with, "What do you mean by attention training?" In some sense, attention is the capacity to be present in your life and receptive to what you are experiencing. These are all in the purview of attention. So, "attention training" or mindfulness isn't training people to be laser focused, or a robot, or mindless drones. Mindfulness practice is really actually doing the exact opposite; it allows your mind to open.

For example, if you are caring for a child, a sick spouse or elderly parent, your attention is focused. On a professional note - an unexpected go-around. Practicing mindfulness on a regular basis creates awareness that opens you up to these experiences. It brings you to the point where you can be more joyful when you are with your child or spouse and more compassionate when you're holding a loved one's hand at the end stage of their life.

Earlier in my life, whenever I was chronically stressed, I would check out. I was not present to my life; it was like being on autopilot. When I was unhappy I was more likely to shout at my children or not respond because I didn't hear or see accurately because I was so lost. One day, I watched my eldest son mimicking me in the kitchen. He was rushing around in a fashion that was all mine. From the kitchen island, to the refrigerator, back to the island, he rushed to place dishes in the dishwasher and all the time talking out loud as if he were me. He was mimicking my autopilot behavior. Another memorable time was when my second son and I were driving in a car together. We were returning from shopping. He was driving the car; I was in the passenger seat. I had worked five all-nighters and was functioning on a total of twenty hours of sleep over five days, which did not put me in a good mental place. I was beyond exhausted. I'll never forget that drive. It was during the drive that he said "something," and it triggered my empty self. I honestly don't remember what he said, and I honestly don't remember what I said, but what I do remember is what I said hurt him deeply. I broke his spirit. I never quite recovered from that event. I realized from these two separate events that I wasn't the parent that I wanted to be. After those two events, I vowed to myself to slow down, to be present to what was unfolding, and to be present to what was difficult as opposed to pushing it away and denying it. I vowed to learn lifestyle skills that would help me discern how to be the parent that I wanted to be.

This experience can also translate into an individual's professional as well as personal life. And this is what I'm most passionate about. What if providing well-being and mindfulness training to pilots would have similar benefits? What's exciting is that feedback and research indicates just that! My own experience in resilience plus the results of scientific studies have made me feel very hopeful. Mindfulness provides more opportunities to practice many skills: leadership, teamwork, communication, situational awareness, decision making, de-escalation, negotiation, and discernment. Individuals are more able to make good choices when they are not in a fog or on autopilot.

All these things happen when cognitive controls are depleted and there are no tools to cope.

One thing that I noticed in my volunteer work with chronically stressed and fatigued pilots was that, even though pilots had a tremendous volunteer-support system, they were still fatigued, drinking too much, experiencing difficulty staying asleep, partaking in substance use and abuse, domestic violence incidents, and facing thoughts of suicide. All these things happen when cognitive controls are depleted and there are no tools to cope.

When bearing witness to their struggles repeatedly, I reached out to our union—and later, to management at my airline—and shared this information. And, even though the company and union promoted and encouraged peer-to-peer groups, I shared that they weren't being utilized enough. I arranged a leadership presentation and introduced the science behind wellbeing and good health which included a sliver of mindfulness training and its benefits. I presented my own stories, and those of others. I posed the questions: What if our pilots could benefit from these well-being and good-health practices? What if, by doing so, safety would improve? Would presenting this information to the rank and file in our yearly LMS program be worth the investment? May there be a chance that well-being, good health, which includes mindfulness training, could be the ninth core component of aviation. Could well-being training be one of the tools in our toolbox—not just some fluffy idea but rather a useful foundational tool to good health?

MIND WANDERING

Dr. Amishi Jha at the University of Miami tells us that psychological stress and fatigue, decreased cognitive functioning, and mind wandering relates to our direct experience when we are feeling overwhelmed. It's typically not because a sabre tooth tiger is chasing us. We are feeling overwhelmed because of the mental content that we generate in our own mind. For example, if we are under pressures such as extended hours at work, trip revisions, weather, diverts, long delays, security checks, line checks, yearly check rides, coupled with financial struggles, relationship struggles, teens, naughty children, caring for aging parents, divorce, insomnia, nutritionally depleted, or chasing a critical deadline, it is those thoughts that are actually the drivers of the emotion that we experience. A cascade effect emerges and composes itself in the experience of chronic stress which leads to chronic fatigue. Our mind wanders. It is biologically impossible to focus when experiencing chronic stress, anxiety, or depression.

The fact that our minds have minds of their own is such a key insight for people. In some sense, mind wandering is the dark matter of cognition. It is constantly having an impact on our cognitive functioning but most of us are not previewed to it. My mindfulness practice is based around the science of mindfulness training. I'm fascinated with the relationship between focusing and having cognitive resources devoted to the task at hand, and then what attention pulls it away.

My curiosity with mind wandering is particularly sparked because of the group that I'm a part of—pilots. By the virtue of our jobs, pilots sit for long periods of time and our mind wanders. What research has found is that mind wandering increases over time. The more time you spend engaging in a task, the more your mind wanders. This is true for many other professions who have to sustain their attention over a period of time. For example, air traffic controllers, a firefighter standing watch, a police officer patrolling, a guard standing watch, or an ICU nurse monitoring equipment. There are so many contexts in which the risk is low—meaning that the chances of something happening are pretty low. But if you don't have your attention present or you don't have the capacity to hold the needed attention for the entirety of time, the consequences can be very high. I think about this every time that I go through a security check at the airport as a civilian. The chances of finding a gun are very low, but TSA—please don't have your minds wandering!

> It is biologically impossible to focus when experiencing chronic stress, anxiety, or depression.

ELEVEN
THE FOUNDATION OF WELL-BEING

So what actually *is* "well-being"? It may be an overused term, but in order to explore well-being, we also need to understand what self-care is, because the two concepts are closely woven together. The *Oxford English Dictionary* defines *well-being* as the state of being comfortable, healthy, or happy.[15] However, it is important to realize that well-being is a much broader concept than moment-to-moment happiness. While it does include happiness, it also includes other things, such as how satisfied people are with their whole life, their sense of purpose, the *quality* of their relationships as well as sleep and relaxation, such as mindfulness meditation, eating nutritious food on the go, exercise and movement.

Well-being begins with silence and stillness. When we listen to our bodies, minds, and hearts, we become aware of deeper motivation, desires, and needs. Realize that to enjoy life, you might need to ease your pace. Perhaps that means adjusting priorities or placing activities that don't bring you joy aside. On the flip side, it may mean making time for people who are easy to be around, who make you laugh, combined with a few minutes of mindful breathing each day. By doing so you will strengthen your instinct to what serves you and what doesn't.

Wellbeing and good health involves more than just eating an orange, taking a relaxing shower, or brushing your teeth. It also includes caring for yourself the way you would care for a child—with consideration and gentleness for your body, mind, and spirit. Self-care or, as some experts call it, emotional fitness, is not taught in school. Therefore, as we evolved into adulthood, we haven't developed adequate tools to develop our emotional fitness.

Emotional fitness can be especially difficult for people who are highly driven. These are folks who are hard-driving, focused, and disciplined to a fault. It also can include caregivers who put the needs of spouse, children, or parents first. In many cases, they've done it for so long that they consider taking care of themselves a selfish act. I had to learn this the hard way. Until my high blood pressure diagnosis, I was entirely unaware that I had put myself last and was running on autopilot, slowly depleting my mind, body, and soul.

Research suggests that people who take care of themselves have more energy to help others, experience increased longevity, and they bring more to their professional role. Think of it like this. An airline can't get 100% from an employee if the employee arrives at work 50% depleted. No amount of training can take the place of 50% depletion. As a result, the more consistently you take care of yourself, the easier it is to maintain a healthy balance between caring for yourself and showing up 100% whether at work or at home.

There are many self-care activities that are part of developing well-being, see the list below for some ideas to start with. These activities cost little or no money, involve minimal effort, and require no new learning. As silly or foreign as a few may seem, they really do work! All you need is to give yourself permission to do them. Start with the ones that speak to you, that you believe will give you the greatest joy or that may possibly tap into your flow. I think you'll find the results immediate and rewarding. What are you waiting for?

- Walk outside and notice nature.
- Go for a leisurely bike ride.
- Hold hands with a loved one.
- Breath in a relaxing essential oil, such as lavender, from an aromatherapy diffuser.
- Drink herbal tea or coffee in your favorite cup in silence.
- Get a massage.
- Call a friend.
- Give a hug to a loved one.
- Listen to an inspirational talk.
- Snuggle with your partner.
- Buy fresh flowers for yourself (even if you're a guy).
- Quiet your mind with relaxation techniques.
- Meditate.
- Give a slow and tender kiss; Be the first to say, "I love you."
- Buy a favorite magazine.
- Pet your dog or cat.
- Eat outdoors.
- Wrap a blanket around you.
- Watch a funny show.
- Laugh at yourself.

Small changes lead to big results. Start by making just one small change a week to benefit your well being and good health. Live with it; cultivate it. By consistently doing small things for yourself, you are better suited to create new neural pathways that will aid you to keep stable during times of stress.

FINDING BALANCE AND RESILIENCE

A Swedish friend of mine shared an insight on balance. The Swedish word *lagom* means not too little, not too much—just the right amount. Lagom is the quality of being sufficient. Adequate. Just right. Enough. There is great wisdom in the pursuit of lagom in our lives. Work and productivity are commendable, but hard work will not make us happy unless it's balanced with exuberant rest, careless play, and joyful love. All of which take time.

It is easy to slide into unbalance without cognitive awareness—it's called habit or on autopilot. There is a strong link between slipping into habit, or autopilot, leaving you feeling stressed or unbalanced when consuming media. Have you ever been aware and noticed your heart rate as you scroll through Facebook, JetFlyer, or any social media platform. There's a pretty good chance you'll see an in-your-face rant of someone. Turn on the television, and there's news about a radical unrest, tension in the Middle East, economic downturn, or violence in a major city. Pick up the newspaper, and there's a story about the latest mass shooting or red skies over San Francisco due to wildfires. All that can have a major effect on throwing us off-balance.

However, once awareness—noticing—is cultivated, the shift begins to a happier, healthier life. This is one small lifestyle change and self-directing step that you can take to improve your balance. One of the many wonderful things about taking steps toward solutions is that they remind us that it is in these small steps that *balance* is cultivated. As you learn to assess, listen deeply and feel the sensations in your body (I feel my stress sensations in my throat), take small steps, and make new habits, you'll start to grow your intuition.

Work and productivity are commendable, but hard work will not make us happy unless it's balanced with exuberant rest, careless play, and joyful love. All of which take time.

Another powerful option to cultivate balance might just be off your radar—letting go. Easier said than done, right? This can be a difficult first step for a few reasons. Letting go can seem difficult because it means letting go of certain aspects of your past and identity that you might be attached to. It also means letting go of your expectations of how things should be and wanting to control situations or outcomes. Some people think that letting go hints of being wrong or allowing someone else to be right. Sound familiar? Any one of these reasons could throw a person's psyche out of balance. Keep in mind your body/mind operates optimally when it's in balance much like a jetliner's center of gravity (CG). In humans this means to balance it takes time to notice, balance, and the willingness to let go.

Resilience

According to Positive Psychology emotional resilience is not about winning the battle. It is the strength to power through the storm and still keep steady. Another way to say this is, resilience is the capacity to maintain competent functioning in the face of major life stressors.[16] Simply put: focus. Here's the catch! If you are struggling with burnout, chronic stress, fatigue, or anxiety, depression it is biologically impossible to focus to perform at the top of your game.

The word *resilience* comes from the Latin word *resilio*, which means to "bounce back" or "retaliate."

The word *resilience* comes from the Latin word *resilio*, which means to "bounce back" or "retaliate."

Emotional resilience is an art of living that is entwined with self-belief, self-compassion, and enhanced cognition. It is the way through which we empower ourselves to perceive adversities as temporary and keep evolving through the pain and sufferings.[4]

In a broad sense, emotional resilience means bouncing back from a stressful event and not letting it affect our internal motivation. It is not a "bend but don't break" trait, rather resilience is accepting the fact that "I am broken" and continuing to grow with the broken pieces together.

Which can be summed up in the Buddhist "mindfulness" philosophy . . . be happy and be useful.[4]

And finally, time—or, more accurately, time off. "One of the greatest labor saving devices of today is tomorrow" is an infamous misquote of Ben Franklin's "Never put off until tomorrow what you can do today." Modern life, alas, follows the mantra "Do more with less," which inevitably and insidiously results in the individual having less time for themselves. WE don't give ourselves the permission to just "be."

It is not a "bend but don't break" trait, rather resilience is accepting the fact that "I am broken" and continuing to grow with the broken pieces together.

The key to mental health and well-being is to develop balance—*lagom*—in one's life. Unfortunately, balancing our limited time is a skill most of us do not learn until it's too late.

TWELVE
BODY-MIND SYSTEM

Think of your body as a whole system. Systems thinking is an approach that views systems in a holistic, integrated manner, rather than isolated components or parts. It examines the linkages and interactions between elements that comprise the whole of the system.

When someone slides into a mental "funk," it's not like fixing a broken leg—we can't just treat the immediate symptoms and expect that person to make a full recovery. Instead, we must see the whole person and all the factors that may affect the system. Systems thinking is particularly useful in addressing complex systems where small changes (habits) in one part of the larger system (body-mind) can lead to large and unexpected effects in the overall system.

For many of us, an overly stressed life is a good example. It's become our new normal. Our culture extols that of achieving, producing, and doing. We rush from one activity to the next, wearing a badge of honor. If we have a brief pause in between, our habit is to fill it with something productive, or else we feel guilty. In this worldview, relaxation is a luxury, an occasional gift that we give ourselves. In a holistic view, relaxation is not an occasional gift you give yourself, it's a key essential component for overall good health.

A constant state of nonstop engagement wreaks havoc on our **nervous system**. Our body reacts the same way to chronic stress as it does to danger. When under threat (either real or perceived), the sympathetic nervous system (known for the "fight or flight" response) flashes signals to our caveman mind (the tiger is chasing me—run!).

During this fight or flight response, a flood of hormones elevates heart rate, blood flow, respiration, along with a cascade of other reactions. Muscles tighten, jaws clench and I see the world through a soda straw. In times of persistent stress, the body's caution and warning system becomes stuck in the *on* position, leaving the body-mind system in a continuous state of stress is an unhealthy, unsustainable situation.

If I'm walking in the woods and look down and see a long, squiggly thing near my feet, my mind instantly reacts—"This is a threat, it's a snake—run!" The body's caution and warning systems go into "override" power, similar to when flying a go-around while on approach to landing. When we realize that this is not a snake, but rather a coiled rope, we take a deep sigh of relief, the sympathetic nervous system disenges and the parasympathetic nervous system engages.

Sometimes referred to as the "rest and digest system," the parasympathetic nervous system conserves energy. When the parasympathetic nervous system kicks in, muscles relax, and heart and respiration rates slow. The caution and warning system (sympathetic nervous system) is turned off.

Because the body-mind is one, stress carried in our body activates the stories in our minds in a search for certainty. This can create a loop with body and mind, thus amplifying the original signal. Our storytelling mind then sends stress signals to our body. For example, if I am at home safely distanced from others during the time of the COVID pandemic, I am in no way at risk.

Should this cause anxiety? The anxiety may feel real. The activation of my caution and warning system is based on a single story that I'm telling myself about the future that may or may not be true.

In the snake/rope example, it was top-down communication, with the brain telling the body what to do. Scientific research has told us that nervous system communication is not just in the direction of the brain to body, it's actually a two-way street. If we intentionally put our body into a parasympathetic state through mindfulness meditation, it communicates to the brain that you are okay. Over time, the brain's gray matter, the part involved in information processing, increases, while the amygdala, the part of the brain associated with the body's fear and stress responses, actually gets smaller. As a result, you are less likely to react in a negative fashion.

Victor Frankel, the psychologist and holocaust survivor, stated that between stimuli and response is *choice*. With continued meditation practice, the space between stimuli and response increases. The tension in the brain, and looping negative thoughts quiets down. For many people, this is enough to interrupt the feedback loop so that the body-mind can relax.

One way to imitate the traits of the parasympathetic response is to pay attention to what it feels like in your body. The breath is an excellent anchor point. Deep breathing relaxes the body and makes it virtually impossible for the mind to remain anxious and tense. It's available to everyone, we do it naturally, we can practice it wherever we are, and it's FREE.

When you breathe deeply, neurotransmitters become regulated. The benefits of deep breathing have an immediate impact on energy levels.

Pausing to breathe brings you into the present moment. Breathe slowly and consciously. Over a period of time, you'll be able to notice the difference and respond rather than react. Whenever I feel an uptick in my stress level, I use the 4-5-7 breath practice to center myself. A former aeromedical doctor taught me this method to reduce blood pressure. I didn't know it at the time, but this was my first exercise in self-regulating breathing, which I now know as meditation.

Whether I'm walking out to the airplane, in an airplane, sitting in my car, or getting ready for a call, I can take a few minutes for this simple breathing exercise— an inbreath for a count of four, hold for a count of five, and an outbreath through the mouth as if blowing through a straw, for a count of seven.

Inhale-2-3-4

Target hold-2-3-4-5

Exhale-2-3-4-5-6-7

With the outbreath, pause and notice and sensations in the body. Can you feel your heart rate slowing?

The deep exhale count is the most important in the tempo since it is here that the heart rate slows down. As your heart rate drops, bring your attention to other sensations that are happening in your body in the present moment. Start out by repeating this exercise three times per day for five minutes, build up to ten minutes, then fifteen minutes a day. This breath-paced parasympathetic reset is one way to bring us back into a place of balance. If you try this and you see no improvement, or on the small off chance that your anxiety gets worse, use this as a self-assessment in self-care. If how you are feeling is not comfortable, or you are just stuck in a holding pattern, it can be helpful to seek a trusted trained professional to talk with.

As you move through life with its compounding concerns, remember to pause, breathe, and check in. Self-assessing, or noticing, is so important. By "checking in" means, you pause and ask, "How am I right now?" Learn to notice, identify, and take action on sensations in your body. Stress and anxiety signal one of two things—either a need of help or a need of self-care.

Self-assessment

Even though some people consider formal mental health services outdated or not in line with how they view their own needs for living well. That's where self-assessing can be useful. In order to achieve well-being, a person needs to continuously self-assess, notice, and take into account all of the factors that may affect their health or happiness.

These factors encompass both internal and external conditions. Internal conditions include things such as thoughts, emotions, beliefs, and behaviors, while external conditions are things like stressors of job and community. There may also be factors such as stressors we may inflict upon ourselves such as alcohol consumption, drug and tobacco use, self-medication, inadequate nutrition, and physiological stress. On the other hand, a person's internal resources such as optimism, resilience and self-esteem, also affects their well-being. But you may be asking yourself "where to start."

Well . . . start here!

How we go about self-assessing and measuring well-being can be challenging, but self-assessing and measuring are still worthwhile. Measuring well-being can be done in a number of ways; there is no one-size-fits-all approach.

Two useful methods are the VIA Character Strengths Survey and Warwick-Edinburgh Mental Well-Being Scale. The Warwick-Edinburgh Mental Well-Being Scale is a scale of fourteen positively worded items, designed to measure both the feeling and functioning aspects of positive mental well-being. For example, the scale included items such as "I've been feeling optimistic about the future," "I've been thinking clearly," and "I've been interested in new things." Participants are asked to choose the answer that best describes their experience of each item over the last two weeks, using a five-point scale. The end result is a score between fourteen and seventy, with a higher score indicating better well-being. The VIA (Values in Action) is a free, fifteen-minute character strengths survey for adults. The measure uses five-point Likert-style items to measure the degree to which respondents endorse items reflecting the twenty-four strengths of character that comprise the VIA classifications (you can visit https://https.VIACharacter.org to learn more). It's the only free scientific survey of character strengths in the world. By taking this survey, you can discover your greatest strengths. Research shows that knowing and using your character strengths can help you: increase happiness and well-being; find meaning and purpose; boost relationships; manage stress and health; and make positive changes to your health.

NERVOUS SYSTEM SUPPORT

Practical training on how to support our nervous system is a hot topic in the science field and a revolutionary approach to help improve the conditions of stress and anxiety. A crucial element is to understand neurotransmitters. Out of the seven major neurotransmitters in the brain, we will focus on three in particular: GABA, serotonin, and dopamine.

GABA is a natural anti-anxiety neurotransmitter. When GABA levels are low, you may feel anxious, remunerative, or obsessive. Serotonin is the natural antidepressant neurotransmitter.

When serotonin is low, you can feel unhappy, have trouble sleeping, and crave things like unhealthy carbohydrates and alcohol. Think of serotonin as being in charge of focus and motivation. When dopamine is low, it can feel hard to stay on track with goals and general routine practices.

People with low GABA often drink alcohol as a way to relax. They qualify their drinking as a way to *wind down* or self-medicate. On the other hand, people with low serotonin say that they drink as *a way to have fun*. People with low dopamine say that they drink as *a way to connect*, and engage with others. The motivations are fine lines, yet the internal feelings are different.

These neurotransmitter deficiencies aren't seen, yet they *do* exist in the body. Pilots who suffer from low GABA **can** stop drinking; it's relatively easy for most goal-driven achievers. However, it is hard to stay stopped, especially if the neurotransmitters that nourish our nervous system are not replenished.

The neurotransmitter dopamine released during pleasurable activities loves creative flow. One of the ways to cultivate creative flow is to focus on a positive activity that ends in *-ing*: gardening, fishing, painting, cooking. There are some activities that end in *-ing* that make us feel like we get a dopamine hit from them, such as drinking, smoking, or overeating, but they are deceptive since they actually *deplete* dopamine.[17]

Have fun with one of these activities listed below:[17]

Climbing	Cooking	Crosswording
Hang gliding	Dancing	Playing handball
Gardening	Fishing	Building
Hiking	Quilting	Drawing
Painting	Singing	Playing the piano
Sailing	Skiing	Snowboarding
Surfing	Sewing	Paragliding Crafting
Scuba diving	Yoga	Painting
Tinkering with a car	Golfing	Beading
Learning a language	Taking flight lessons	Woodworking

It's okay to learn and take part in an activity in which you don't need or want to invest a lot of time and energy, unless you are ready for a bigger step. The process is what is therapeutic. What crosses my mind for me personally is the game of golf. I don't have to do it well. I am just the dancer, and the game of golf is dance. Perhaps cooking is what brings out your creative side. It doesn't have to be overly involved. Enjoy!

THIRTEEN
SUCKED IN BY SOCIAL MEDIA

Google knows your interests. That's not by accident, but rather, by design. What I want people to know is that everything they are doing online is being tracked, watched, monitored and recorded. A lot of people think Google is just a search engine, and Facebook is just a place to see what friends are doing. What they don't realize is there are entire Silicon Valley teams of engineers and software creators whose job it is to use your psychology against you. An embarrassingly heavy social-media habit isn't entirely your fault. Pinterest, Facebook, and Twitter have all been designed to make you repeatedly use them and check back in. The software system is using our psychology against us and it's negatively affecting humanity like never before.[18]

In the Netflix documentary, *The Social Dilemma*, creators and inventors bare their souls and take us back behind the curtain of social media. The documentary reveals that the creators have used psychology against us, and explains how social science works. Social media affects our kids, and everyone around us. It changes what you think, how you think, what you do, and who you are.

In essence, what the internet industry has created is a market based on the question of "How much of your life can you give us?" Our attention is the product.

Harvard Professor Zubo said, "This is what every business has dreams of. To have a guarantee that if it is placed in an 'ad,' it will be successful." That's their business. They sell certainty. In order to be successful in that business you have to have great predictions. Great predictions begin with one imperative thing - data. When you keep in mind that technology is designed to hold your mind hostage, you might be motivated to set time limits and take small steps. This is a new type of market place that has never existed before. It's a marketplace that trades exclusively in "human futures," just like there are markets that trade in pork belly futures or oil futures. We now have markets that trade in human futures at scale. And those markets have trillions of products, the trillions that have made the internet companies the richest companies in the history of humanity. They have more information about us than has ever been imagined in human history—it's unprecedented.[18]

Taking steps to reduce our exposure to technology is vital to our overall mental health and well-being. Vow to stay off social media or to not check your phone during meals or when family and friends are present. Give your mind the freedom of unplugging. Consider signing off for a weekend once a month. If this is a huge step, try a Saturday, and then add Sunday. A one-day pause isn't enough to break a habit, but it's long enough to trigger ideas for better habits. You'll still be anxious when you return to the onslaught of electronic emails or text, according to Larry Rosen, PhD, the author of *iDisorder*. But a little time away from the screen reminds you how nice life is without push notifications and status updates.

Be a discriminating editor when it comes to your posts and notice the content that you tend to share on social media. Before you post a status update or a photo, question your motive. Are you just trying to prove that you're having a good time? Don't get sucked into this rabbit hole. Is this the tenth selfie, or foodie that you've posted this week? If the answer is yes, try texting the picture to only the meaningful people in your life. Connecting offline with people is becoming a lost art. Calling a person on the phone and letting them hear your voice, or sending a handwritten note via old-fashioned mail may make someone's day.

FOURTEEN
NEW HABITS, NEW PATHWAYS

The research is solid: Healthy relationships with others is another key to reducing stress. Close social bonds and community have a direct impact on our nervous system. In our technology-driven world, compounded by isolation due to the 2020 COVID pandemic, we have become very deficient in human touch. Make time for touch! Do you get massages? Or the hands-on energy work Reiki? The particular modality doesn't matter, pursue what resonates with you. Human touch is essential to keep your mentally, emotionally, and physically in balance. Muscular tension can occur as an automatic reaction to uncomfortable thoughts and stress. Massage helps muscles relax. Letting go of accumulated muscular strain is key to overall stress, anxiety, or depression relief. Give hugs! Research shows that getting five hugs a day for four weeks increases happiness. Hugs, especially long ones, release oxytocin, the love and bonding hormone. Physical touch has an immediate impact by boosting the neurotransmitters GABA, serotonin, and dopamine.[4]

Gathering with others with the intention to connect and practice rituals is nothing new—as humans, we all yearn for connection: to be seen, appreciated, and loved. But there seems to be a need, now more than ever, to craft these intentional spaces with the people in our lives. Regulating gatherings are a long standing spiritual tradition, from the Jewish Shabbat dinner on Friday nights to Christian church services on Sunday mornings. In the Buddhist tradition, a sangha is a local community of mindfulness practitioners who gather to meditate and to encourage each other on the path of practice. It doesn't matter what you do; just bring your *attention* and set an *intention* to connect with people for the purpose of deepening presence and connection, establishing connections and making community with friends, family, and others who are like-minded and inviting them to gather. Make it official—designate a place, day, and time to come together. Your meeting up can be weekly or whatever works. You can make it a routine, a new habit, or host a gathering online. Intentionally set a time and day to gather and bond—order a few large vegetable pizzas and some adult refreshments! It'll be fun and therapeutic.

Close relationships, especially within families, can be fraught with friction, testing our tolerance and willingness to **forgive**. Holding onto grudges and anger is damaging to the individual who clings stubbornly to these toxic emotions. Resentment is like drinking poison and expecting another person to die. Nelson Mandela was once asked by an interviewer, "How does a man spend twenty-seven years in prison, put there by an oppressor, and come out of that experience with not a heart of stone, not a cold heart but a heart that is willing to forgive and embrace?" The interviewer also reflected upon one night over dinner when Mr. Mandela profoundly stated, "That our hatred for the oppressor was so intense we did not see the value of talking to him." The reporter continued, "At what point did you see the value of letting go of the hatred and begin the process of talking again?"

Mandela's response was this: "That is a great tragedy to spend the rest of your life in prison, but although it looks ironical there are advantages. If I had not been to prison, I would not have been able to achieve the most difficult task in life and that is changing yourself. I had the opportunity because in prison you have what we don't have in our work outside of prison. The opportunity to sit down and reflect."

Could this be you? Be honest with yourself, and consider forgiving those who may have wronged you. But by all means, don't forget to also forgive yourself.

Nutrition

Good nutrition plays a crucial role in maintaining well-being and good health. The great news is that there are specific foods and lifestyle practices that help facilitate healthy neurotransmitter balance. Food is medicine. Consuming quality fats, protein, and organic produce provide amino acids and nutrients that are the building blocks of neurotransmitters.

The B vitamins found in leafy greens play a key role in cell development and renewal and are the precursors to serotonin, which helps reduce the risk of depression. It is a good idea to minimize your intake of animal products since these are sources of unhealthy fats. But if you love your meat and cheese, there are healthier choices to make.

The quality of the animal products you consume counts. When animal protein comes from pasture raised ranches and farms, there is a definite difference in taste, and the meat is leaner and contains healthy fats. It also provides higher qualities of protein and nutrients such as creatine and carnosine for muscle and brain health.

Grass-fed beef and lamb from Australia contain higher amounts of vitamins A and C and other antioxidants. Grass-fed animals and their eggs contain much less monounsaturated fat, up to five times more beneficial Omega-3 fatty acids, and twice as much Conjugated Linoleic Acid (CLA), a natural trans fat that occurs in many healthy foods.

Investigate to learn if the animal products you consume have been raised responsibly and sustainably. Poultry and their eggs should be pasture raised or free range. Full-fat dairy from grass-fed/pasture-raised cows, goats, or sheep is best.

The actual nutrients in pasture raised animals' diets will vary due to the different plants they consume. Therefore "eating local" is particularly important in maintaining your overall health, not just for your vegetables, but all your food, including animal proteins. You will notice allergies will lessen as you build up antibodies eating food that is locally grown and raised and your overall health will greatly improve.

As with all things, moderation is best. Just because a food is labeled certified organic does not mean it is healthy for everyone. **Read labels and follow your health provider's guidelines on the amount of meat and types of food that are healthy for you.**

LOVE YOUR LIVER

There's nothing wrong with a happy hour beer or a glass of wine for dinner. But when that one glass of wine turns into two nine-ounce glasses, then the danger is that, over time, it turns into a bottle. To keep physical and mental health risks low, limit your alcohol intake. For men, the recommended intake is two drinks per day (for example, a twelve-ounce beer being one drink), for women, the recommended intake is one (for example, five ounces of wine being one drink). Consuming more than the recommended amounts of alcohol might make you fall asleep, though it can't keep you asleep. "Alcohol fragments sleep," Breus says. "You may feel drowsy at first, but then you'll wake up for a long period between REM cycles."

Did you know that alcohol is processed through the liver? Think of the liver as the filter for your body. Keeping a healthy liver is vital to achieve overall health. The liver is the second largest organ in the body, and does more than just filter out toxins. It also processes nutrients from your stomach and intestines after digestion. A *plant-based, whole food* diet is the best type of food to detox your liver. To detox your liver, you will need to put the meat back in the freezer, hide the refined sugar, cut back on caffeine, and limit or cut your alcohol consumption for a couple of weeks and get a refresher on the food colors of the rainbow.

Here are ten foods to add to your diet to help cleanse your liver:

1. Purple beets—Naturally cleanse and purify the blood, boosting liver function. Beets are high in antioxidants, pectin, fiber, and iron. The fiber in beets flushes toxins out of the body, as opposed to being reabsorbed in the bloodstream.
2. Cruciferous vegetables—Cauliflower, cabbage, bok choy, kale, watercress, radishes, brussels sprouts, and broccoli are all low calorie, high fiber, and contain glycosylates, which produce enzymes that aid in the removal of toxins and aid in digestion. Broccoli also is a good source of vitamin E.
3. Sweet potatoes, carrots, pumpkin, and butternut squash—All are anti-inflammatory and contain beta-carotene, which converts to vitamin A. They are also high in vitamin C and fiber.
4. Lemons—Naturally cleansing and full of antioxidants and vitamin C, lemons are initially acidic, but alkalizing once metabolized by the body; and they are a natural replacement for salt.
5. Lentils—This easy-to-digest legume is full of fiber and a natural source of plant-based protein.
6. Healthy fats—Avocados, olives, ground flax seed, coconut, walnuts, and pumpkin seeds are healthy fats. Most nuts are considered good fats. Peanuts are a legume, not a nut, and therefore is not a healthy fat. Try to avoid plant oils (vegetable, canola, peanut, or safflower oils) as they interfere with bile production, which also affects the digestion of fats. Small amounts of olive oil and coconut oil are the exception.

7. Apples—Apples are full of fiber, and remove toxins from the liver and blood. Granny Smith apples are the highest in malic acid, a naturally cleansing nutrient that also removes carcinogens from the blood. Apples must be bought organic, as they are heavily sprayed with pesticides.
8. Garlic—Rich in allicin and selenium, powerhouse nutrients for your liver. Allicin helps facilitate a strong immune system, and selenium is a natural detoxifying mineral.
9. Onions—Rich in allicin, potassium, fiber, phytonutrients, and flavonoids that help your body fight off the common cold as well as repel toxic chemicals.
10. Dense organic leafy greens—Spinach, kale, chard, romaine, arugula, and collards are some of the densest leafy greens and are packed with chlorophyll, which purifies the blood, and helps neutralize heavy metals, toxic chemicals and pesticides. Consuming organic leafy greens prevents adding toxic chemicals back into your liver.

The main or key ingredient of all these vegetables (except for lemons and healthy fats) have in common is fiber. Lemons and healthy fats provide the liver with enzymes that speed up the digestion, neutralize toxins, and excrete waste. Add these with the fiber benefits of the other vegetables and you are well on your way to achieving a healthy liver and a healthier life. For best results, buy these ten groups of vegetables local (within a 100-mile radius), organic, and in season.

Looking for tasty ways and recipes to prepare these plant-based foods? There are many social media groups, websites, and healthy food apps online. Check out the Happy Cow, Vanilla Bean, and Food Monster apps. When you eat the rainbow and choose organic, local, seasonal foods, you are giving yourself a valuable gift.

When you are on the "road," keep these items in mind. I'll be the first one to admit that it's not easy to find nutrition in airports, airplanes, and pricey hotel restaurants, but it's not impossible. Hot meals on short layovers aren't going to happen either. I live by the 80-20% rule: Eighty percent of the time, I'm eating clean at home; and when I work, I'm eating the other 20%, but still keeping eating "clean" in mind as best as I am able.

KEEP MOVING - EXERCISE

The science behind movement of any type is very clear. Exercise is beneficial in reducing stress and gaining self-control. Regular exercise gradually builds lasting physical strength.

Any physical activity, just moving can initiate a boost in neurotransmitters. Exercise does not have to be over-strenuous or boot camp style. Going for a brisk walk, walking up a set of stairs versus taking the elevator are small examples that yield big results. Interestingly enough, Boston University conducted a study with yoga. After the class, participants were tested, and it was found that everyone's GABA in the class went up at least 27%. Some even had an 80% rise in GABA compared to a control group that read a book for sixty minutes.[19]

However, after we are active, we need to be still. Stillness allows the sympathetic nervous system to respond in a nourishing way through adaptation to the complex world in which we live and work. Sitting in stillness and silently invoking mindfulness meditation or prayer is where we feed and replenish our GABA, serotonin, and dopamine.[19]

THE FOUR-LEGGED SOLUTION

What does a miniature goat have in common with a cat? Or a potbelly pig with a miniature horse? What does a dog have in common with tropical fish? These animals can all be used to help calm anxiety and help people to regain peace and their quality of life.

In the past, animals only had one job—to work. Dogs herded livestock, cats caught mice and rats in the barn, goats kept the weeds down, and horses were used for transportation. In the last 150 years, animals have been recognized as greatly beneficial for helping people recovering from illness, surgery, or the loss of a loved one. Animals can also help people with disabilities, such as blindness, deafness, or someone confined to a wheelchair.

Any animal can be used as a therapy animal, but dogs are usually the preferred species. You see therapy dogs in places such as hospitals, courtrooms, medical offices, schools, and on airplanes!

Animals are helpful in easing psychological disorders by affecting the mental health of those around them in positive ways. I'll use dogs as an example, however, a cat or any similar kind of pet will give you the same benefits.

Here are some ways that having a pet will emotionally benefit you and your family:

1. They help ease anxiety. Dogs are great at picking up on their human's anxiety. They will come sit next to you and anxiety subsides as you cuddle them.
2. They make you take responsibility. When you don't want to get out of bed and face the world, dogs depend on you to feed and take care of them. When you take your dog outdoors for a walk, your mood changes. The fresh air and sunshine works wonders alongside your dog that loves and depends on you.
3. When you are lonely, your dog will be there for comfort. They love us and want to be near us.
4. Dogs quickly become our best friend; they make us happy. They understand our cues and moods. They can tell when we

are sad or happy. They understand us, and yes, they can even communicate with us!

5. Dogs keep us healthy. They can improve our heart health by keeping us exercising regularly. When you take your dog out on a walk, you will find your stress levels going down. Petting your pet helps reduce blood pressure.
6. Dogs do not judge their humans!
7. People who suffer from PTSD find that when they have a pet, their brains release endorphins, the "feel good" chemicals so they are able to focus on the present, rather than negativity and past trauma.

With one in five people suffering from mental illness, the benefits of having animals around help with stress, anxiety, and depression. Interacting with animals can increase your oxytocin hormone levels. Oxytocin is our "feel happy" and "I trust you" hormone, which explains how we bond with our pets. There may even be long-term benefits in terms of our health.

"Oxytocin has some powerful effects for us in the body's ability to be in a state of readiness to heal and to also grow new cells, so it predisposes us to an environment in our own bodies where we can be healthier," said Rebecca A. Johnson, PhD, RN, FAAN, FNAP, professor and director of the Research Center for Human Animal Interaction, College of Veterinary Medicine, and the Millsap Professor of Gerontological Nursing, MU Sinclair School of Nursing, University of Missouri.[20]

"The majority of research projects studying the effects of Animal Assisted Therapy have been small, but most indicate that this kind of therapy has great potential in the mental health field," said Kathleen Doheny.[21]

NATURE

A wonderful way to nurture well-being and good health is to take a walk in nature. You don't have to climb a mountain to appreciate nature; it's actually all around us. All you need to do is slow down, be mindful, tune into your senses, and walk through nature with an intention to hold in awareness all that surrounds you. Being in nature reduces stress, anxiety, and depression. Researchers who have published studies in *Environmental Health and Preventive Medicine* journals found that cortisol levels (stress hormone) and heart rate decreased for people who spend time in nature.[22]

Spending time outdoors is not only beneficial physically, but also improves one's state of mind and mental resilience. All around the world, people look for opportunities to connect with nature. Forest therapy refers to immersing yourself in the forest to experience the natural environment with all the senses. Forest therapy is a type of mindfulness practice that involves noticing and sensing the present moment rather than ruminating about the past or future. The benefits of forest therapy is partly due to phytoncides, the essential oils that emanate from plants. Phytoncides improve immune system functions by increasing the number of white blood cells, the fighter cells in our body kill viruses and tumors. These airborne molecules, along with antifungal and antibacterial agents that protect trees from insects and disease, are available for all of us, and they're free!

FIFTEEN
SLEEP IS YOUR SUPERPOWER

I'm often asked how I overcome stress. My response wasn't the kind of thing that you might expect. It wasn't hot yoga, Pilates, hydration, or nutrition. Don't get me wrong, those are all important, but my number one priority for overall well-being and good health is *sleep.* There's nothing more valuable to my body and stress recovery than sleep. It's so crazy that sleep is the most powerful thing you can do for your immune system. Like breathing, sleep is the most natural thing you can do to take care of yourself.

Sleep disruption is often one of the first signs that a person is feeling stressed.[23] In turn, lack of sleep exacerbates stress, so it is important that pilots deal with sleep issues as soon as they arise before a negative pattern develops.

A recent study at UC Berkeley revealed that men who sleep less than four hours per night have testosterone levels of a person ten years older than their chronological age.[23] This reminds me of the time when I began working with my functional medicine doctor. She had performed non-traditional blood tests and we were ready to review the results. I'll never forget the appointment. She sat in front of me and stated, "You may look okay on the outside, but your cell age says something different. It indicates that your cell health is one of an eighty-year-old woman." I sat in my chair in disbelief. At the time, my age was fifty!

Another interesting fact in the Berkeley report is that learners need sleep before and after the learning event to commit information to memory. The study participants were divided into two groups: a sleep group and a sleep deprived group. The sleep group got eight hours of sleep, while the deprivation group was kept awake at with no naps or caffeine allowed. The next day, participants were put in an fMRI scanner and asked to learn a list of new activities while images of brain activity were recorded. Afterwards, participants were tested to see how effective the learning was. What they found is not surprising. The sleep-deprived group exhibited a 40% deficit in their ability to learn or recall information.

This is concerning for people who perform night shift work. The Berkeley study further discovered that people who are well rested versus sleep deprived process signals from the hippocampus (the informational files of the brain) significantly differently. The sleep group received new memory files, while the sleep deprivation group exhibited zero new signals.

Healthy sleep habits are very important to develop and keep. Let me share with you my sleep habits to give you a sense of how I make it a top priority. My sleep hours are scheduled. I make sure that I get a minimum of eight hours of quality precious sleep. This can be challenging for airline pilots, but then again pilots are good at challenges. I take a relaxation and meditation break for one hour every day. I break the hour up in twenty- to thirty-minute increments. Sometimes this means a quick catnap; sometimes it means sitting in silence, resting, or breathing. Relaxation doesn't mean surfing the web!

My day revolves around my sleep schedule when I'm at home. My target bedtime is 9–10 p.m. and I wake up naturally between 6 a.m. - 7 a.m. Does that mean I hit my target every night? Most nights—yes! I absolutely do not compromise those seven to eight hours of sleep. I create a sanctuary with no distractions. When I'm on the road, hotel room accommodations can be challenging. As an airline pilot, I'm all so familiar with hotels changing from night to night, but my sleep condition needs do not change. A comfortable bed is critical, with the right pillow being the key.

Make sure the temperature is optimal, for me it is 65–70 degrees. I completely block outside light with blackout curtains and take a coat hanger with clips from the hotel room closet and clip the curtains closed. Another trick is taking the ironing board from the hotel closet and leaning it against the window treatment, keeping the curtain opening closed. And I put a towel over anything that emits light such as clocks or electronic devices and also place a rolled up towel under my hotel door to reduce loud hall noise.

Many people discover that consuming information on mobile devices an hour or two prior to bedtime contributes to restlessness and an inability to fall asleep (blue light). It's tempting to check social media or "open time" for the umpteenth time before bed. Think of winding down to sleep as an airplane coming in for ILS or RNAV approach to land. The airplane loses altitude and speed as it comes in for a safe and soft landing. The same holds true for stimulus reduction before you are able to fall asleep; the body-mind system doesn't shut off like a toggle switch. I turn off all electronics at least forty-five minutes before going to sleep. No iPhones, no iPad, or anything that might keep my alertness engaged.

PRIORITIZE SLEEP

Adequate sleep is one of the most natural and best gifts you can give yourself, your family, and your organization. If we want to maximize our health and longevity, pilots need to cultivate good psychological and physical habits both on the job and at home. Making sleep a priority is a challenge that takes time and commitment. To prioritize sleep, we need to push back on literally everything else in our life—work schedule, responsibilities, relationships, projects, friends, and family. The moments of any given day are limited, and time is precious. If we want to make the most of our time, prioritizing is critical.

No matter if I am at home or on the road, I'm always planning my stress recovery, with sleep a priority at the top of the list. Some people believe that sleep is a sign of laziness. They try to glorify how they run on five hours of sleep, or how they can sleep anywhere, as if that ability was a badge of honor. Or they might boast, "I sleep when I get tired." Well, that may be true, but consider this: When you're on an international trip, your body clock is still in the time zone you departed from—where you live! So, picture this: Your body clock is telling you that it's time to sleep, you're tired and you are scheduled to meet your colleagues in the lobby in an hour for a fourteen-hour trip back to the United States. What do you do in that case?

How does "I'll sleep when I get tired" truly work for you now? We all like rhythm, and so do our bodies.

According to Berkeley sleep scientist Matt Walker, sleep deprivation is terrible for the brain, but it also affects our bodies. The cardiovascular system is negatively impacted by a lack of sleep. In the study at a global experiment researchers across the globe were startled to discover that when people lose an hour of sleep every spring converting to Daylight Savings Time, there was an increase of heart attacks by 24%. Conversely, gaining an hour of sleep in the autumn led to a 21% reduction of heart attacks.[24]

Where you fall on the enough-sleep/sleep-deprivation spectrum contributes to the state of your immune system. For everyone, but especially as we get older, it is paramount to keep your immune system as strong as possible. One of the best things you can do for your immune system is sleep. Did you know that when we sleep there are so-called "killer cells" that come out and increase the strength of our immune system? Think of them as protective gear. When we don't get enough sleep, killer cells are not present to afford protection when our bodies need them most.

This same study of the global experiment revealed a 70% drop in natural killer cell activity for one night of sleep that was restricted to four hours of sleep. That's a concerning state of immune deficiency. Research is now finding the risk of cancer of the bowel, prostate, and breast is so great that the link to night work has been classified as a probable carcinogen because of the disruption of your sleep rhythm.[24] Have you ever heard of the saying "You can sleep when you're dead?" On a serious note, it is mortally unwise advice. The simple truth is, the shorter our sleep, the shorter your life. The time we have is precious and so is the time we sleep. It restores us in every way. The way that I think about it is that every minute I spend sleeping is like putting a deposit in the savings account jar. If I put one minute in, I get back two minutes of me at my best. What a great return on investment.

YOUR SLEEP AFFECTS OTHER PEOPLE

The most considerate thing you can do for people around you is to be healthy and present for them. Your airline, colleagues, friends, and family depend on you. Nothing is more important in those relationships than you being happy, healthy, and balanced. If you are thinking, "This isn't for me," consider this: If you're trying to push yourself to do more, be more—if you're trying to get the most out of your time, to be as creative as energetic as you can be, to show up fully present in the world and at work every day—then you need to recharge your system.

If you want to seize the day, you have to sleep at night. Night sleeping is where your body recovers, replenishes, and renews. Sleep is not an optional luxury, but rather, a non-negotiable biological necessity. It's your life's support system. An epidemic of sleep deprivation is having catastrophic effects on our lives.[23] It is time to reclaim your right to a full night's sleep without apology. When we do, we are reunited with the elixir of health.

I would be remiss to ignore the reality that some of you out there are night flyers and international flyers. That is a problem when it comes to your overall health longevity. However, if it's just the way it is, it is what it is. If so, it's time to demand from your union, your company, that work schedules must reflect time to recover. Otherwise, the job becomes a hazard and public health danger. This is no different than workers not being told—or given tools—to remove asbestos from a building safely. Or coal miners who, after years of employment, have a greater risk for black lung disease, yet the organization did not equip them nor explain the dangers to the jobs was to their health. Providing tools to help keep pilots healthy is partially the responsibility of aviation organizations. Healthy pilots mean healthy airlines.

There was a time early on in my career where I sacrificed sleep for my family. I've learned over the years what a mistake that was. When my children were school age, I would fly the night shift. I was lucky, because where I resided was near where the airplane laid over. At the time, I stayed a first officer because it allowed me "quality of life." Don't get me wrong: it did, but at a cost. I landed at 5:30 am, just enough time to drive home and get the kids up for school, pack lunches, offer them breakfast, and kiss them good day! After they were off to school, I would lie down in my bed and maybe get four or five hours of sleep. I did this for almost twenty-five years!!! My family was such a priority to me that the risk to myself was disregarded in the pursuit of being at home during the days for my children.

After my *aha* moment at age fifty, when my blood pressure skyrocketed and anxiety was high, one thing was for sure: my sleep had to improve. No more night hub turns for me. From that moment on, sleep became a resource that I protected at all costs. I know now that if I don't get enough sleep, it will impact every part of my body. There is simply no feature of your well-being that retreats at the sign of sleep deprivation and lets you get away with it.

Circadian rhythm disruption

Night shift work can cause circadian rhythm sleep disorders. When an individual's body clock becomes desynchronized from its accustomed wake/sleep and light/dark cycles, insomnia and/or daytime sleepiness results.

It is also important to realize that the impact of circadian disruption is not a linear problem. After several days, depending on the individual, we seem recovered. The reality is that almost every different organ has its own recovery rate. For example, the liver can take up to two weeks to recover from jet lag (this is straight-up recovery, not alcohol-related recovery). What happens if you are doing week on week off international flying? Your liver is in a constant state of flux. With its prominent role in so many areas of your health and health maintenance, that can't be good.

Those of you who have done the hub turn / red-eye-to-a-dead-head trick must now realize that you are doing real damage. There is more to the effects of circadian and diurnal disruption than just fatigue.

Any sleep during the beginning, middle, or end of the night is better than sleep during the day. You may feel worse for a short time, but there is a clear benefit of a thirty-minute nap. Lastly, the obvious—sleep at night as much as possible, keep long breaks between international trips and rest when you can. Will that stop the damage being done? No, but until we have more definitive studies and the union negotiates better work scheduling practices to include these considerations more aggressively, you must do what you can.

When my last son went off to college, I decided to up my exposure in the international flying theatre. As an international pilot, sleep is always challenging. One of my tricks and tips to mitigate the stress on my body was to keep my body in an eastern coast time zone +/- one to two hours. I chose trips that would line up with my priorities, sleeping and eating, +/- one hour to keep my digestion happy.

On an interesting note, there have been studies of people that seem to do well doing shift work. Their bodies seem to make some adaptation, so not everyone is impacted at the same rate or severity. While they may seem less affected daily, there is no correlating information as to longevity.

Hormonal change

Some important questions have been raised for the aviation community regarding the effects of diurnal and circadian disruption on the human hormonal systems. Let's not sugar coat this. The effects are serious and need to be understood if pilots, air traffic controllers, flight attendants are to mitigate the negative impact on their lives. There's a lot to unpack. My experience is to make connections between and correlations that have not been studied and therefore are anecdotal in nature, based on research, through experiences and interviews. It is important to note that research defining the scope and impact of hormonal disruption has increased dramatically within the last twenty years. This book only scratches the surface. There's a lot more to unpack. Let's begin.

Our physical strength is expressed through our muscles and skeleton, our function and performance rely on our brain driven nervous system. This is one of the reasons why B vitamins and replacing neurotransmitters in the brain are so important. On the other hand, our vitality and health are driven by our endocrine system (hormones).

Our endocrine system is a complex overlapping system of hormone release and inhibition that manages our body temperature, energy use, blood glucose level management, cell growth and replacement, and immune system function, among many other things. The impact of pilot lifestyles and schedules can be devastating to these key systems. Some of this may be a bit technical, however, the importance of this information will be clear as you read further.

In November 1998, *The Journal of Environmental Medicine* reported, "The airline industry may be an occupational setting with specific health risks. Pilots tend to experience debilitating effects of erratic time changes resulting from jet lag due to international flying and radical shift changes of domestic flights." Other factors to be considered, as the article continued, "are circadian disruption and conditions specific to air travel, such as noise, vibrations, mild hypoxia, unregulated atmospheric pressure, low humidity, and air quality," are concerning. The article continues stating, "US pilots have experienced significantly increased mortality due to cancer of the kidney and renal pelvis, motor neuron disease, and external causes. In addition, increased mortality due to prostate cancer, brain cancer, colon cancer, cancer of the lip, buccal cavity (mouth), and pharynx was suggested."[25]

Since these studies were printed, there have been several studies, including the Nurses' Health Study, that have shown a clear connection between circadian/diurnal disruption and increased cancer rates as well as increased cancer growth rates during exposure to disruptive schedules.[25]

There is now increasing research into the impact of chronic fatigue. This early study clearly identifies potential health risks: "Chronic sleep debt has been linked with the disruption of numerous modulators of immune function including SMS hormones, HPA hormones, and cytokines (Vgontzas and Chrousos, 2002). However, the potential role of immunosuppression associated with chronic sleep debt has received little attention."[26]

PART III
TIME FOR ACTION

SIXTEEN
FREEDOM TO SPEAK

The aviation community considers well-being as a key to safety and efficiency. In the book *Human Factors in Flight*, author Frank Hawkin's discussion regarding the primary definitions of Human Factors said, "Its twin objectives can be seen as effectiveness of the system, which includes safety and efficiency, and *well-being* of the individual."[27]

It's not difficult to see how stress affects safety and efficiency in the cockpit. Since we all experience stress on a spectrum due to external and internal conditions, it's not humanly possible to remain balanced at all times. People don't develop problems overnight. The earlier people get honest with themselves that they are having difficulties coping, the easier it is to recognize, identify, and label behaviors, then take the big step and *reach out to professionals who you trust.*

Anxiety often will have close arms to depression. Chronic stress can stay hidden for years, manifesting as general anxiety. Symptoms most likely will not show up at the same time, but can be related at one time or another. It takes an average of eleven years for a person to seek help. Pilots can become aware that they have a problem after a series of events, but can't risk the step to self-report. A person doesn't have to hit "rock bottom," using or abusing substances, but this behavior can slowly chip away at physical and mental well-being.

In the meantime, pilots keep quiet until they cannot function anymore. Sometimes they are "found out," and then they run around with their hair on fire. Others go out on medical leave when they reach the point when they perceive that there are no other options available. They feel out of control.

However, there is a small group who waits a long time and then finally reveals the truth to the world. For our generation of pilots, mental health comes with a stigma. It's tricky because we are still left with the question of how. Talking about our struggles could put us in the state of "not operationally qualified"(NOQ), or potentially, if we are honest, lose our job. It's a catch-22. Safety is at risk if we don't talk, and our livelihood is at risk if we do. How do we reconcile this dilemma from which there is currently no escape due to mutually conflicting conditions?

SEVENTEEN
HEALTHY EMPLOYEE = HEALTHY BUSINESS

It is not a secret that Google takes great interest and pride in their employees. When I was in my course work at UC Berkeley, I met Larry Green, Heath Performance and Global Service lead at Google. Larry explained that in the last decade, the benefits of working at Google have become legendary. Google employees enjoy perks that are unheard of in many corporate environments, including above and beyond health benefits, onsite restaurant dining, free books, bowling and arcade machines, and rest and recreation areas. What Google knows is that its all-encompassing benefits are good for the business as well as the individual. What the organization gets is that an employee with a healthy body/mind means a healthy organization.

Let's take a look at how other Fortune 500 companies are focusing on the wellbeing and good health of their employees.

A case study is Aetna—an insurance company whose reported income in the third quarter of 2018 was in excess of $15.0 billion. Mark Bertolini, now CEO, suffered severe injuries and almost died. Mark's story is not only compelling and inspirational, it is said to be miraculous. While skiing with his family in Vermont, his 6'1" frame ricocheted off a tree and over a ledge sending him careening thirty feet down a ravine. Air lifted to the local hospital, Mark was given his last rights. Somehow, he miraculously pulled through.[28]

Months later, he continued to experience debilitating pain and was put on a cocktail of OxyContin, Vicodin, and Fentanyl. They barely helped. A year later, he began looking into alternative therapies. Craniosacral therapy, a modality that improves the circulation of spinal fluid got him off narcotics in four months. To improve his wrecked flexibility, he grudgingly turned to yoga, and then mindfulness meditation.[28]

Through his healing journey, he convinced his top medical officer, Dr. Reismam, to consider programs such as yoga and mindfulness for Aetna employees. Initially Dr. Reisman laughed at Mr. Bertolini idea. Dr. Reisman said, "Marc, just because you're doing yoga doesn't mean we all need to do yoga." With convincing advice from Mr.Bertolini, Dr Reisman eventually agreed to consider endorsing it for their employees. But before that, he wanted to see data. With test results in hand, Dr. Reisman finally agreed to approve the yoga and meditation in the organization. Mark also reached out to the American Viniyoga Institute and eMindful, a Florida company that teaches mindfulness via videoconference. Mark wanted to evaluate if his employees would benefit from the same practices in which he had. To bring academic credibility to the project, Mark reached out to Duke University's Integrative Medicine Program which has grown adept at tracking the benefits of alternative treatments. They set up shop on both their East and West Coasts for testing.[28]

After twelve week of tests, the results were revealed. All the employees who kept with either yoga or mindfulness reported a significant reduction in perceived stress and sleep difficulties. They also show improved breathing rates and heart rhythm coherence, a measure of autonomic balance. Here's the amazing part. There was also evidence that these programs might impact Aetna's bottom line. Compared to the controlled group, the employees who saw their stress drop had lower overall health care costs, to the tune of $2,000 per employee per year.[28]

Since the initial study, Aetnas has offered mindfulness, yoga, and several preventative wellbeing programs to more than a third of its employees. In fact, workers who engage in these courses also showed similar gains in self- reported measures of time management, perceived strenuousness of their jobs, mental and interpersonal demands at work, and their ability to handle their workloads better. It also made them more productive and efficient. Before taking the Mindfulness at Work course, employees were losing 146 minutes per week in productivity. After completing the program, the amount of lost time was reduced to seventy-seven minutes.[28]

Another example was published in the journal of *Occupational Health Psychology* in 2012. The authors shared a concise refresher on just how mindfulness in the workplace works. "Mindfulness may reduce stress by allowing individuals to significantly shift their experience by learning to pay attention in the present moment, with a curious and accepting attitude," they reported. "By training the mind to notice a stream of sensory and perceptual events, one begins to realize how intention and behavior are formed. The careful and repeated practice of this nonjudgmental observation gradually allows individuals to realize that events are actually unfolding processes that can be quite fluid. In other words, even apparently negative events, thoughts, sensations, emotions, and behaviors come to be seen as changeable. While this process is not necessarily conscious even in those learning it, the process does allow individuals to experience the world in a significantly different, and less stressful way."[28]

EIGHTEEN
AWARENESS AND EDUCATION

Given the cost benefit and employee moral benefit experience at Google and Atena, what can the airlines and industry learn from these two independent examples? Equally importantly, pilots, their families, and labor organizations need to be better educated about the prevalence of, and possible safety complications due to the lack of pilot mental and emotional fitness.

An Embry-Riddle Aeronautical Scholarly article discusses, expands, and highlights pilot mental health initiatives. DeHoff and Cusick stated the International Civil Aviation Organization (ICAO) and the FAA revisited recommendations to ensure safety. The FAA did so through the establishment of the Pilot Fitness Aviation Rulemaking Committee in May 2015. ICAO and FAA initiatives were supported by independent organizations also seeking answers into pilot mental fitness. The most notable of these reports came from the Aerospace Medical Association, a group of aviation medical professionals dedicated to industry safety and human performance that has expertise in the field of psychology.[8]

So far, so good, right? Here's the catch: It's also recommended research and the establishment of clear guidelines and regulations for medical professionals and outlined the obligations to report mental illness to aviation regulatory bodies that supersedes patient confidentiality rights.

It is clear that current regulations need to change in order for pilots to speak freely about their mental health. It's no longer acceptable to have the existing aviation medical assessment process in place with additional emphasis on common and less severe mental illnesses (such as stress, anxiety, and depression) unless pilots can speak freely without jeopardy to their livelihood.

Organizations need to embrace and introduce programs that raise the awareness of not only physical health, but also the mental health of its pilots. In turn, safety will be improved. It is a waste of time to advocate for measures to improve rapport between pilot and medical examiner through lifestyle questions about stress, mood, and sleep. Acknowledgement of stigmas and cultural barriers of mental health issues are meaningless if a pilot can't be assured that he or she is not risking their job to talk about mental health.

The bottom line is this: We need to do more to remove the barriers, fears, and penalties surrounding mental illness in the aviation industry so pilots are more likely to self-report, get treatment, and return to work.[29]

Closing Thoughts: Finding Solutions

So, what can organizations and industry do to address the stress, anxiety, and depression that the aviation community is experiencing? Let's circle back to Google and Aetna. What are they doing that we can learn, adopt, and execute? The Pilot Fitness Aviation Rulemaking Committee released their final report in November 2015. There were eight regulatory recommendations, the following two caught my eye:[30]

- Air carrier operators should be encouraged to implement mental health education programs for pilots and supervision that improve awareness and recognition of mental health issues, reduce stigmas, and promote available resources to assist with resolving mental health problems.[30]
- Encourage advocacy for a uniform national policy on mandatory reporting of medical issues that affect public safety.[30]

I think that we all can agree that the promotion of positive mental health and well-being for good health is a force for good. According to behavior therapist Ben Companion, "Government agenda repeatedly endorses and promotes positive mental health and well-being agenda."[31] We have begun to look closer at this concern in the United States. But it's not enough.

Excerpts from the current FAA stance on mental health is as follows:

- Certain medical conditions such as psychosis, bipolar disorder, and severe personality disorder, automatically disqualify a pilot from obtaining an FAA medical certificate and prohibit them from flying.[8]
- However, many pilots have conditions that are treatable. Several United States airlines already have reporting and monitoring programs that provide the pilot with a path to report their condition, be treated for it, and return to the cockpit once the FAA has determined—through a rigorous evaluation—it is safe to do so. It's important to highlight that the FAA addresses these cases / medical certificates of pilots on a case-by-case basis.[8]
- The FAA will issue guidance to airlines to promote best practices about pilot support programs for mental health issues. The FAA will also ask the Aerospace Medical Association to consider addressing the issue of professional reporting responsibilities on a national basis and to present a resolution to the American Medical Association.[8]
- Airlines and unions will expand the use of pilot assistance programs. The FAA will support the development of these programs over the next year. These programs will be incorporated in the airline's Safety Management Systems for identifying risk.[8]
- The FAA will also work with airlines over the next year as they develop programs to reduce the stigma around mental health issues by increasing awareness and promoting resources to help resolve mental health problems.[8]

(The above information may be found at the Pilot Mental Fitness Fact Sheet: https://www.FAA.gov/news/fact_sheets/news_story.cfm?newsId=20455.)

In a paper published in *International Journal of Aviation, Aeronautics, and Aerospace*, DeHoff and Cusick state that dismissing possible mental health challenges can undermine aviation safety. It points out the many examples of unsafe or even deadly actions by pilots suffering from mental health problems. Some include life-threatening or potentially life- threatening events as I've discussed earlier in this book. However, compromised safety includes seemingly benign occurrences that, while they don't pose an immediate lethal threat to passenger or crew safety, may contribute to errors that ultimately compromise safe operations.[8]

What we know for sure—based on a survey of over 6,000+ pilots—is that there is overwhelming evidence that pilots are under extreme stress and public safety is in their hands. The current legislation may help drive pilots underground as aviators are forced by the regulatory environment barriers to decide whether to seek help at the risk of being grounded. And once grounded, the lawyers descend as pilots work to get reinstated to flying status. Safety is enhanced when well-being and mental health is addressed, as opposed to allowing pilots to go uneducated, undiagnosed, and untreated. It's up to the FAA to mandate that industry follows the recommendations once the regulation is addressed.

Review Inquiry

Hey, it's Reyné here.

I hope that you've enjoyed the book, finding it both useful and meaningful. I have a favor to ask you.

Would you consider giving it a rating wherever you bought it? Online book stores are more likely to promote a work when they feel good about its content, and reader reviews are a great barometer for a book's quality.

So, please go to the website of wherever you bought the book, search for my name and the book title, and leave a review. If able, perhaps consider adding a picture of you holding the book. That increases the likelihood your review will be accepted!

Many thanks in advance,

Reyné O'Shaughnessy

Will You Share the Love?

GET THIS BOOK FOR A FRIEND, ASSOCIATE, OR FAMILY MEMBER!

If you have found this book valuable and know others who would find it useful, consider buying them a copy as a gift. Special bulk discounts are available if you would like your whole team or organization to benefit from reading this. Just contact Reyne@Piloting2Wellbeing.com or visit https://www.CaptainReyneO.com.

Would You Like Reyné to Speak to Your Organization?

BOOK REYNÉ O'SHAUGHNESSY NOW!

Reyné accepts a limited number of speaking and training engagements each year. To learn how you can bring her message to your organization, email Reyne@Piloting2Wellbeing.com or visit https://www.CaptainReyneO.com.

Endnotes

1. Hoffman, W., N. Chervu, et al. "Pilot's Healthcare Seeing Anxiety When Experiencing Chest Pain." *Journal of Occupational and Environmental Medicine*. 2019;61(9): e401-e405.
2. Hoffman, W., D. Barbera, J. Aden, M. Bezzant, A. Uren. "Healthcare related aversion and care seeking patterns of female aviators in the United States." Archives of Environmental and Occupational Health. 2021. DOI: https://doi.org/10.1080/19338244.2021.1873093
3. Wu, A., D. Donnelly-McLay, M. Weisskopf, et al., "Airline pilot mental health and suicidal thoughts: a cross-section descriptive study via anonymous web-based survey," *Environmental Health*, 2016, 15(12): 1–12.
4. Bor, R., C. Eriksen, M. Oakes, and P. Scragg (Eds.), *Pilot mental health assessment and support: A practitioner's guide* (Routledge/Taylor & Francis Group, 2017).
5. "Depression," World Health Organization, January 30, 2020, https://www.who.int/news-room/fact-sheets/detail/depression.
6. Wu, Alexander C., Deborah Donnelly-McLay, Marc G. Weisskopf, Eileen McNeely, Theresa S. Betancourt, and Joseph G. Allen, "Airplane Pilot Mental Health and Suicidal Thoughts: A Cross-sectional Descriptive Study via Anonymous Web-Based Survey,"

Environmental Health, online December 14, 2016, DOI: 10.1186/s12940-016-0200-6.

7. Mental Health Commission of Canada, https://www.MentalHealthCommission.ca/English.
8. DeHoff, M. C., and S. K. Cusick (2018). "Mental Health in Commercial Aviation – Depression & Anxiety of Pilots," *International Journal of Aviation, Aeronautics, and Aerospace, 5*(5). Retrieved from https://Commons.erau.edu/ijaaa/vol5/iss5/5.
9. Sickel et al., *Mental Health Stigma Update: A Review of Consequence* (https://Commons.erau.edu/ijaaa/vol5/iss5/5).
10. Bor, Robert and Todd Hubbard, *Aviation Mental Health: Psychological Implications for Air Transportation* (Burlington: Ashgate Publishing Company, 2006), pp. 137–138.
11. Pilot Medical Solutions, Inc., 2016; Aeromedical Consultancy, 2016; FlightPhysical.com, 2016.
12. Airline Pilot Forums, 2016; *Flyer*, 2016; Pilots of America, 2016; Jet Flyer, 2017.
13. International Federation of Air Line Pilots' Associations, 2012; Air Line Pilots Association, 2016; European Cockpit Association, 2016.
14. Langshur, E. and N. Klemp, *Start Here* (New York, NY: North Star Way, 2016).
15. *Oxford English Dictionary*, 2nd ed., Oxford University Press (1989).
16. Kaplan et al., "What is emotional resilience and how to build it," *Positive Psychology* (1996), retrieved from https://PositivePsychology.com/emotional-resilience/.
17. Hays, P. A., *Creating Well-Being: Four Steps to a Happier, Healthier Life* (Washington, DC: American Psychological Association, 2014).
18. McDavid, Jodi, "The Social Dilemma," *Journal of Religion & Film*, vol. 24, no. 1, 2020, p. COV41+. Gale

Academic OneFile, link.gale.com/apps/doc/A616580373/AONE?u=anon~68857ff0&sid=googleScholar&xid=2c39b9ac. Accessed July 5, 2021.

19. Boston University, "Researchers Identify Link between Decreased Depressive Symptoms, Yoga and the Neurotransmitter GABA," BU School of Medicine, February 3, 2020, https://www.BUMC.bu.edu/busm/2020/02/03/researchers-identify-link-between-decreased-depressive-symptoms-yoga-and-the-neurotransmitter-gaba/.
20. Quote by Rebecca Johnson. Bauer, Amber, "Why Do Pets Make Us Feel Better?", *The Cancer.Net Blog*, April 23, 2015, https://www.Cancer.net/blog/2015-04/why-do-pets-make-us-feel-better.
21. Doheny, Kathleen, "Pets for Depression and Health," 2012, www.WebMD.com/depression/features/pets-depression.
22. Yau, Katherine Ka-Yin, and Alice Yuen Loke, "Effects of forest bathing on pre-hypertensive and hypertensive adults: a review of the literature," *Environmental Health and Preventative Medicine* 25,23 (2020), ISSN: 1347-4715. https://EnvironHealthPrevMed.biomedcentral.com/articles/10.1186/s12199-020-00856-7 https://doi.org/10.1186/s12199-020-00856-7.
23. Anwar, Yasmin, "Lack of sleep shrinks men's testicles?" UC Berkeley, Wednesday, May 22, 2019, https://www.UniversityOfCalifornia.edu/news/lack-sleep-shrinks-mens-testicles.
24. Walker, Matt, "Sleep is your superpower," updated on December 13, 2020, TED Talks Daily, https://Smashnotes.com/p/ted-talks-daily/e/sleep-is-your-superpower-matt-walker.
25. Schernhammer, E. S., et al., *Journal of the National Cancer Institute* (October 17, 2001), Vol. 93, No. 20, p. 1563–8. Journal Code 7503089. ISSN: 0027-8874.
26. Sephton, S., and D. Spiegel, "Circadian disruption in cancer: a neuroendocrine-immune pathway from stress to disease?"

Brain, Behavior and Immunity. October 2003, 17(5):321-8. DOI: 10.1016/s0889-1591(03)00078-3. PMID: 12946654.

27. Hawkins, Frank H. (Author), and Harry W. Orlady (Editor), *Human Factors in Flight*, 2nd ed. (Brookfield, VT: Ashgate Publishing, 1987).
28. Michael Chaskalson, *The Mindful Workplace: Developing Resilient Individuals and Resonant Organizations with MBSR* (Wiley-Blackwell, 2011), ISBN-13: 978-0470661598.
29. Federal Aviation Administration, *Guide for Aviation Medical Examiners* (2016), https://www.FAA.gov/about/office_org/headquarters_offices/avs/offices/aam/ame/guide/.
30. Pilot Fitness Aviation Rulemaking Committee, November 2015, https://www.FAA.gov/regulations_policies/rulemaking/committees/documents/media/Pilot%20Fitness%20ARC%20Report.11302015.pdf.
31. Quote by Ben Companion, 2017.
32. Rory Carroll, "Warning over pilots' mental health as planes return to skies," *The Guardian*, June 2, 2021, https://www.TheGuardian.com/business/2021/jun/02/pilots-mental-health-planes-covid-airlines.

Resources

After more than a decade of self-administered practice, I decided to pursue a teaching certificate in Mind Based Stress Reduction (MBSR) at Brown University, a public health university known for its academic rigor (visit https://www.Brown.edu/Public-Health/Mindfulness/Classes to learn more about their programs; you can also learn about becoming a certified health coach through Integrative Functional Medicine Academy which is an approved health and wellness coach training program by the National Board for Health & Wellness Coaching (NBHWC).

I recommend that you start with baby steps, forming new pathways, but keep in mind that it may take more than your own will to get this train back on the track. If you feel that you need some help, consider reaching out to a wellness strategist. I love working with people to create a safe space where they are truly seen and heard and am honored to walk with them on a path to well-being.

METHODS

- Mindfulness Based Stress Reduction (MBSR)

- Mindfulness Based Cognitive Therapy (MBCT) / Cognitive Behavioral Therapy

  Compartmentalizing emotions, anxiety, and depression may be a reasonable short-term solution in an emergency, but as a long-term strategy, it doesn't work well. Imagine running your engine as hard as you can—despite the warning lights on your dash. Mindfulness and meditation practice, along with cognitive behavioral therapy and positive psychology, have become beneficial practices in managing stress and emotions. The three practices done in tandem result in remarkable results.

- Mindfulness Based Attention Training (MBAT)

  Dr. Amishi Jha is an associate professor of psychology at the University of Miami whose research on attention, working memory, and mindfulness has explored and clarified the neural bases of executive functioning and mental training, using cognitive neuroscience techniques.

  You can read about some of Dr. Jha's findings in "The Brain Science of Attention and Overwhelm" (here is a link to the full article: http://www.Mindful.org/Youre-Overwhelmed-And-Its-Not-Your-Fault/).

  For more information on The Jha Lab, visit: http://www.Amishi.com/Lab/.

  The Jha Lab has been conducting Mindfulness Based Attention Training or MBAT with the United States military for years. In one study, Navy Special Forces teams were given MBAT training pre-deployment. Some of the individuals took the training seriously and developed a regular daily practice, while others weren't interested and gave it little attention or chose to skip it. Once deployed in the Middle East, those who had no interest in MBAT training noticed something surprising: Those who were practicing mindfulness were sleeping regularly, and they were not. So they contacted The Jha Lab and asked if they could do the MBAT training while actively deployed. The results were positive and impressive.

For an interesting interview with Anderson Cooper, Dr. Jha, and Major General Walter Piatt, click here: https://www.YouTube.com/watch?v=pN64uJlRasI.

- Positive Psychology

Positive psychology turns traditional psychology on its head by shifting the focus from individual problems and weaknesses to human strengths and potential. Positive psychology is primarily a research-oriented field that includes a wealth of studies pinpointing the elements of and contributors to happiness and well-being, including the role of relationships, meaning, and purpose.

The new wave of positive psychologists seem to understand kindness, generosity, humor, optimism, courage, hope, and other positive qualities, experiences, and conditions. Some of their findings contradict long held beliefs about what makes people happy.

The Mindful Aviator

The big question now for aviators around the world is "Can MBAT training be useful in improving performance, safety, SAA, resilience, and quality of life for airline pilots?"

We at Mindful Aviator are developing answers to these questions with scientific research. Beginning in 2021, our team of five airline captains, Dr. Amishi Jha of the Jha Lab, and the Human Factors department at Embry-Riddle Aeronautical University will begin a series of studies to determine the effectiveness of MBAT training on commercial pilots.

For more information on who we are and what we do, check out the Mindful Aviator website: www.MindfulAviator.com

— Reyné O'Shaughnessy

About the Author

Captain Reyné O'Shaughnessy is the founder of Piloting 2 Wellbeing, an aviation specific based wellbeing organization that builds on her thirty-four-plus years of experience as a commercial airline pilot. Recently retired, her experience includes B747, B727, Airbus A300/310, and B767/B757 aircrafts and has logged over 10,000 hours of jet flight time. Reyné has over a decade of experience as a health and wellbeing strategist and she has earned a facilitator certification from Brown University in Mindfulness Based Stress Reduction (MBSR) in addition to her BS in Leadership and an Executive Certificate in Business from UC Berkeley. She helps others in high-performance professions achieve a healthier, more rewarding life using practical techniques. Reyné is a visionary leader who brings a clear idea of what a healthier, stronger future for aviation professionals looks like; she writes more about this in her book, *This Is Your Captain Speaking*.

Reyné can be reached at: https://www.CaptainReyneO.com.

Made in the USA
Middletown, DE
19 November 2023